BASIC CARP FISHING
Peter Mohan

Also by Beekay Publishers:

Coarse
Carp Fever by Kevin Maddocks
Success with the Pole by Dickie Carr
Pike Fishing in the 80's by Neville Fickling
Tactics for Big Pike by Bill Chillingworth
Modern Specimen Hunting by Jim Gibbinson
Fishing for Big Chub by Peter Stone
Top Ten edited by Bruce Vaughan
Redmire Pool by Kevin Clifford and Len Arbery
Cypry the Carp by Peter Mohan

Game
The Colour Guide to Fly-tying by Kevin Hyatt
Robson's Guide. Stillwater Trout Flies – an
Alphabetical Survey in Colour by Kenneth Robson

Sea
Long Range Casting and Fishing Techniques by Paul Kerry
Dinghy Fishing at Sea by Phill Williams and Brian Douglas

(Catalogue sent free on request)

First published 1982
Reprinted 1985
BEEKAY PUBLISHERS
103 Worcesters Avenue
Enfield, EN1 4ND

©Peter Mohan 1982

Printed and bound by
Castle Cary Press Limited

ISBN 0 9507598 5 6

CONTENTS

The author with a near-20lb common.

Acknowledgements

My grateful thanks for help with this book go to my good friends and BCSG/CAA colleagues Roger Emmet, Kevin Maddocks and Ron Middleton; to Kevin again for all his hard work in taking most of the photographs; and to Alan Whibley for his excellent line drawings.

* * * * *

Most of the tackle used in this book was bought from Veals of Bristol, where I normally get my tackle. The tackle bag is by Terry Eustace, all the reels are Mitchells, the bait and bait materials came from Duncan Kay's Angling Services, and the flavours are by Geoff Kemp. The carp sack and weighing sling are from Kevin Nash.

Introduction

This book is intended mainly for those who are just taking up carp fishing from other branches of angling. Most anglers do this without any planning and with little knowledge of this specialised branch of angling. If they follow the ideas set out in this book, they should soon become carp anglers, or at least they will have some idea of the best baits, methods and rigs to use for carp when they do go fishing for them.

Carp fishing is not for all; a special type of temperament is needed, and those who have this, and who have read this book, should be well on the way to becoming specialist carp anglers. They will find that carp fishing is not as difficult as they had thought, provided they choose the right waters and the right methods.

Read in conjunction with 'Carp Fever', by Kevin Maddocks, also a BK Publishers book, which is more comprehensive, it should give as complete a picture as possible of modern carp fishing.

One advantage of writing a book is that the author can put in and leave out whatever he thinks to be right. Obviously I have not included everything connected with carp fishing in this book; it would have been impossible to do so. I have, however, put in all that I think is important to those who are taking up carp fishing today; all omissions are intentional!

I have spent 35 years carp fishing, 16 years organising the British Carp Study Group and the Carp Anglers' Association and many years editing and publishing more than 60 carp fishing magazines, and this is my fifth book about carp and carp fishing; if the book helps others to enjoy carp fishing as much as I have done over the years, I am amply rewarded: if not, I can, at least, claim to have tried.

Peter Mohan, February 1985

1 Starting

In my opinion, there are two levels at which you can approach carp fishing: either you want to be able to catch carp while at the same time spending much of the time fishing for other species, or you wish to become a carp specialist with most, if not all, your time being spent carp fishing.

Whichever course you decide on, I am going to assume, for the purposes of this book, that you will wish to be as successful as possible, while you are actually fishing for carp. Even if other species remain your main interest, it is well worth learning how to succeed on your comparatively few carp trips, so my first piece of advice is to fish only for carp on carp fishing trips, and to forget about other fish. Never fall into the trap of using one rod to fish for other species whilst your carp rod 'fishes for itself', a practice which is adopted by many non-carp anglers when carp takes are few. When a take does finally come, you are likely to miss or lose the fish if your full attention is not on the carp rod, so fish both rods for carp and learn to put up with the lack of activity for the sake of the excitement when a carp is hooked.

This advice is not necessary for those who are only interested in carp, but both types of anglers need a systematic, methodical approach while they are carp fishing, and before they start, if they are to succeed. I know most of the leading carp anglers in the country, and one of the main things they have in common is this degree of methodical planning of their fishing. I am therefore going to suggest an approach for the beginner which will almost certainly not fit in with the ideas of many who read this book! I believe, however, that those who take this advice and start in this way will almost certainly be well on the road to success, although to be a carp specialist a certain type of temperament is needed;

if you do not have this temperament, you might well be advised to concentrate on occasional carp fishing trips amongst your general fishing; if you do have it, then you are already well on the way to successful specialisation in carp fishing.

Although it is difficult to define temperament, the true carp specialist is not necessarily a patient person, but he must be able to endure long periods of inactivity without losing his concentration to any marked degree, while at the same time he must be able to think clearly and act quickly, without panic, during those often frantic minutes after the carp takes, is hooked, and the fight begins. You can only find out if you have the right sort of temperament by going carp fishing, but if you follow my plan it will, I believe, help you to develop the right approach from the start.

1. READ

Before you go carp fishing, look at carp lakes or even buy your tackle, start by READING all you can about carp and

Never despise the small carp. Fish like this 8lb scattered mirror will teach you a lot in your first season.

carp fishing. Ignore those who tell you you can't learn by reading. Those who say this are usually people whose ignorance of carp and carp fishing often astounds me even after they have had several years as carp anglers, and it helps to explain their lack of success.

There is now plenty of carp fishing literature; read, and preferably buy, rather than borrow, all the books on carp fishing you can; then join the CAA to obtain the magazines as well. Attend as many meetings as you can, when you will learn plenty from fellow members.

2. CHOOSE YOUR WATER

This is the most vital first step you can take, and the one over which most mistakes are made. You need to begin by *catching* carp, even if they are small, not just fishing for them, so you must try to find an 'easy' carp water; there are more about than you might think. Don't choose the nearest lake to your house, nor the local big fish water where experienced carp anglers spend long periods catching large, hard-to-catch fish. It may cost you more, but will be well worth it in experience, even if you have to do quite a lot of travelling to reach that easy water. More people have given up carp fishing, having failed to catch much, because they chose these hard waters than for any other reason—I even know of people who have spent hundreds of hours carp fishing in waters which contained *no* carp, simply because they were told by others that big carp had been seen, or caught, from the water! Remember, we are *planning* our fishing methodically, so after having read and learnt as much as you can absorb about carp fishing, your planning should now extend to finding that heavily stocked carp water where plenty of carp are caught.

Start by enquiring in all the local tackle shops for waters, getting details of all local clubs which control waters containing carp; read the adverts. in the angling press and get details of all mentioned and advertised carp waters within, say, a 50 mile radius of your home. Finally, get the Ordnance Survey maps for the area, make a list of the locations of every lake or pond, however small, visit it, and find out from people who live locally whether it contains carp, and how you can fish. Questions to anglers fishing, and locals, should soon give you some idea of how often the carp are caught, but *never* believe what you are told—a very cynical outlook, I know, but it will save you wasting much time—just use the information you obtain from talking to people, combined with what you can see for yourself, to assess the potential of the waters you find. If you see lots of carp being caught, or are able to see large numbers in the water, then you are in business. The easiest carp waters are the hungry ones, where there are too many carp for the amount of food in the water; the fish won't grow big, but if they are short of food, they will be easy to catch.

Carp-only waters are best, of course, followed by those in which carp are the main species, with mixed fisheries with a small head of carp least important on your list. I would suggest no more than two waters to fish at first, and one is better as long as you are catching from it. From a water of this kind, perhaps only containing carp to 8lbs or so, I think you should set yourself a first season target of 100 fish. If you can catch this number in a season, even if most are only 3 to 4lbs you will have obtained a lot of experience in striking takes, hooking, playing and landing fish, while in most heavily stocked waters of this kind you can expect to see a lot of the fish, which will help you to learn much about their behaviour in the water. If the water is clear, and especially if you can catch them on surface baits, you will be able to observe how the fish react to a bait, and even how it is taken. Make no mistake about it, if you can learn in your first season to be successful with these small carp, converting as many takes as possible to fish landed, then you are not likely to have much difficulty in landing larger fish.

A final point on water selection, which I cannot emphasise too strongly: be prepared to travel, even if the cost means you have to give up something else to afford the money to do so, rather than to settle for the lake 'just down the road', simply because it is easier and cheaper to fish, even though it is of the wrong type. If you are lucky, you will have an easy water near you; if not, then travel.

If, perhaps for reasons of disability, lack of transport etc., you find it impossible to travel far—and very little is impossible if you are prepared to give up enough for it, or to take enough trouble—then you may *have* to settle for the nearest water, even if it is hard, but you may soon become discouraged if you catch little. To give an idea of what can be done, a young friend of mine found such a water as I have described about 40 miles from his home. At the age of 15 or so he used to travel each way, by bus, with all his tackle, for two hours, with a walk of over a mile at the end of the bus ride, and the same on the way back—4 hours in the bus, a two mile walk, and the last bus left at 7 pm! He also had to use all his money for bus fares, and not for other purposes—this might entail cutting down on the beer and fags for older people!—but he thought it worth while—and so it was; having started with 100 or so carp to 8lbs in his first season, he went on to become one of the best carp anglers in the country. YOU can do the same, or just succeed at a more occasional level, if you follow the 'Mohan plan'.

Just a double; Peter Mohan displays a nicely marked carp.

3. BUYING TACKLE

Now that you have the carp knowledge from reading, and you know the sort of water you are going to fish, you can go out and BUY YOUR TACKLE (not buy it first, as so many do).

Get the sort of tackle to suit the water and fish you are going to catch in your first season, though if it is chosen well, it will be useful for the future. Since most of these easy waters are small, you will not have to cast far, and the sort of compound or medium taper rod you see me using in the illustrations will be right to start with. 10ft 6ins to 11ft — I prefer the shorter lengths, as many of these small carp waters are surrounded by trees and bushes—of 1½ to 1¾lb test curve, of fibre glass, which can be used successfully at distances of 6 yards to 60 yards. A Mitchell 300 or 406 reel, or one with a similar sized spool, line of 8lbs BS for open waters and 12lbs for snaggy or heavily weeded water—I suggest Maxima or Sylcast, size 4 eyed hooks (I use Richard Walker Carp Hooks, but Au Lion d'Ors are very popular), and Arlesey bombs, swivels and artery forceps will be needed. A landing net with 36in arms will land even a 30 pounder, though you can go up to 42in arms if you think you will be fishing open water for big fish later, a tackle bag, a comfortable chair, and some bite indicators and rod rests is all you need—I will give more detailed information on tackle later.

You do *not* need to go off and buy the very latest in electric bite indicators, although judging by the letters I get, many beginners do this even before they get their rods! After all, I've managed without any sort of 'buzzer' for 34 years and over 3,000 carp! However, for anything more than a few hours fishing, at night, and in waters where takes are small, a 'buzzer' is recommended; it may well help you to catch more fish with its useful early warning when your attention may be wandering.

Now, I know what some of my readers are thinking—in all his methodical and detailed plan, he hasn't mentioned the most important aspect of carp fishing today—bait. The omission was deliberate; I do not think that bait is anything like as important as many other aspects of fishing, and it is rarely important at all in the sort of water where you are going to start your carp fishing. However number 4 is: **BAIT**. In the type of water I have suggested for starters, bread, luncheon meat and sweet corn will probably catch. If not, you can move on to trout pellet paste and proprietary baits such as Duncan Kay's 'Slyme'. High protein baits, most of which are based on casein or sodium caseinate, are not likely to be needed.

Nowadays, just about everyone who takes up carp fishing has heard of high protein baits, which they seem to think are something magical, to the extent that this is nearly always the first thing they ask about; one recent correspondent even asked me to send him some ingredients to make these baits—he must have been short of money! If you have chosen your first water correctly, you can almost certainly forget HP baits: bread, luncheon meat and sweet corn will almost certainly catch carp in the easy waters. In Red Beck lake, one of the six waters which I run as carp fisheries, anglers who have never caught carp before are getting 10-15 carp a day, and every one is being caught on the three baits mentioned above. I had 11 carp in 1½ hours there recently, all on floating crust in the evening, with the best fish just over 10lbs. Easy waters do exist, you see! This is a season ticket water near Evesham, Worcestershire, which contains only carp and trout, and there are often vacancies.

Use cubes of luncheon meat—Bacon Grill is very good, and if using sweet corn don't attempt to hide the hook—carp cannot recognise hooks, and top carp specialists catch twenty and thirty pounders with the baits mounted on the shank or eye of the hook, with all the rest exposed.

If your easy water doesn't respond to one of these baits, it will be surprising but if, after a number of trips, you cannot catch, you are not likely to need to go further than cat food or trout pellet paste. Just mix a tin of pet food—Kit-E-Kat is good—with a stiffener such as flour or breadcrumbs until it becomes a (very smelly) paste—or get trout pellets (often available from pet food shops such as 'Pond Pride') and put boiling water on them (about one third of a pint of water to a pint of trout pellets is usually about right), then leave to cool and knead into a paste. If it doesn't stay together, add a stiffener such as flour until it does.

If you can't catch on one of these five baits, then YOU are doing something wrong—or you haven't chosen an easy water after all! Or, more likely, you haven't tried for long enough—persistence is essential in carp fishing. However, if all these baits do fail, then you will need to try medium protein, HP or HNV baits (see Bait chapter).

5. And now—**GO CARP FISHING**! Put into practice all you have read about, and learn from your mistakes—and, indeed, from your successes. Do not be easily satisfied. If you are missing fish, experiment with bait hooking, baits, bite indication, striking methods etc. until you are hooking every fish. If you lose fish, work out why. Never get miserable or discouraged—just try harder. Get into the habit of doing as the really expert carp men do, and spend every bit of 'thinking' time analysing your fishing, trying to work out the reason for any failures, and what you need to do to achieve success. Don't *accept* failures—they are almost always your fault! If you get broken, it is a failure — it should almost never happen. Only recently I saw one of the angling papers praising a big catch of carp by an angler; had he not lost and been broken by as many fish again, they said, he would have had double the weight of fish! This is not success; it is bad angling. You are there to land fish, not to lose them, and if revised tackle, heavier line, or anything else is needed to land those fish, then you must use it. The angler who boasts of the big fish he has lost is a bad angler; what counts is getting them on the bank in as sporting a way as possible without much risk of leaving hooks and line attached to a lost fish's mouth.

You should now be fully prepared to catch carp, but keeping to the methodical approach, you still need a fishing plan. The first aspect of this should be to go as often as you can, and to fish for as long as you can. Then try to learn to 'read' the water—find out where the fish congregate, both

10¾lbs—a target for the first season perhaps, but don't worry if you never reach it, as long as you catch plenty of carp.

to feed and to lie up; find the depths and note the features of the water; where the fish can be caught quickly and easily; and to find out, by trial and error, the times when you can catch fish, and to fish at these times as far as possible. When you are an old fogey, like me, you can perhaps afford to go when it suits you, and to refuse to fish, as I do, at times which are inconvenient for you. However, when you are starting you may have to put yourself out a bit if most of the carp on your chosen water are caught at unsocial hours, although this is less likely in the easy, hungry waters on which you are going to start.

Obviously, I am not saying that it is essential to do things in exactly the same way, and in the same order, that I have suggested, but if you do work to a well thought out plan from the start, rather than just getting a rod and going fishing anywhere, I am sure you are more likely to become a successful carp angler.

Even if you are not a beginner, but have done a season or two without much success, it might well pay you almost to start again along the lines I have suggested. I know it works, because I have suggested something of the same kind in books and articles before, and have heard from many anglers who have told me that this sort of approach has transformed their carp fishing. I hope it is of help to you.

In the following chapters, I intend to expand on each of the subjects raised in this first section, and to go into more detail which will also, I hope, be helpful.

2 Attitudes & Approach

1.

Not long ago, I had a letter from a novice carp angler who complained that other anglers made fun of him, and denigrated his catches when he did get anything; then he went on to admit that carp fishing terms meant nothing to him, and that he knew 'very little about it!'. He had started carp fishing without taking the trouble to learn anything about it —would you take up golf without knowing what 'par', a 'birdie' and an 'eagle' mean?

Read all you can lay your hands on, but don't necessarily expect all the 'experts' to agree about everything. If you come across conflicting advice, then do what you think is best, but in most basic carp fishing topics you will find the experts agree.

Start, of course, by absorbing all the information in this book, including the glossary of carp fishing terms at the back of the book. Once you know these, you can at least *talk* like a carp angler, and so avoid being laughed at by those who think they know it all.

Then join the CAA, read the magazines—not taking too much notice of the advanced articles—and come to CAA meetings and Conferences, where you will learn plenty from our speakers and from conversation with others.

Once you have got as much background information as you can remember, try to ensure that you are going to have a positive attitude to your fishing. You are going to succeed; you can catch those carp—and you will. Of course, you will not find out whether you have the right temperament to make a good carp angler until you start fishing. In carp fishing in most waters, there will be long periods with no action, followed by short frantic minutes when everything seems to happen so quickly that you will need to be able to react almost automatically to what happens.

If you find that you can stand the inaction without being too bored, yet avoid panic when a fish is hooked; if you avoid getting too upset when you lose a good fish at the net, which happens to us all at times and that you can enjoy even your blank sessions, while at the same time thinking out ways to avoid them, then you probably have the right temperament for carp fishing.

If you get fed up quickly, you must have action every few minutes, and you lose fish through not staying calm when they are hooked, then it might well be better for you to keep to only occasional carp fishing, as mentioned in the first paragraph of this book.

Be confident, but be ready to learn from anyone and anything which happens during your fishing, or at any other time, for that matter, Now, armed with your theoretical knowledge and the right attitude to your carp fishing, you are ready for the next step.

The waiting game; do you have the temperament for it?

2. Choosing Your First Water

If possible I advise starting on one water only, but it MUST be the right sort, and you can find it by the means which I suggested in Chapter One. It should be heavily stocked with carp which are easy to catch—the size of the fish is not important. It is better to travel quite long distances, even if you can fish much less, to find this type of water, rather than to settle for that hard, big-carp water just down the road, where you will spend your season catching very few fish, and not gaining experience of striking, hooking, playing and landing carp which you need.

Once you do find the water, learn as much as you can about it before you start to fish, by asking locally and talking to, and observing, those who fish there. Generally, there is no difference whatever in hooking and landing carp of 7lb, 17lb or 27lb. If you learn to do things the right way with the small fish, you will have no difficulty when you get into the bigger ones—in fact, the smaller carp quite often fight harder! The struggle of a really big carp can sometimes be disappointing.

If you find it quite impossible to discover an easy water, you may have to settle for the most productive one available, and try to fish it more often to compensate for the fact that if it is a harder water, you will not catch so many fish.

Do the whole of the first season on the easy water, unless by about half way through the season you have already caught a hundred or so carp, in which case you could spend some of your time at a slightly more difficult place, where the fish are larger. However, if possible I should keep this until your second season.

On discussing this with Kevin Maddocks, head of BK Publishers and one of the country's leading carp anglers, I find that the sort of easy, small carp water I have been writing about is not common in the south east. Carp anglers in this part of the country may have to settle for the 'average' club or day ticket water, where they may catch fewer, but larger, carp.

They may also find themselves starting, not with single rods and quick takes from hungry fish on floating crust, but legering at 20 to 60 yards with two rods, using meat, TP paste baits, or proprietary baits from the beginning. If this is so, they should reduce their target for the first season to perhaps 50 carp, but try to catch as many as possible for experience.

However, easy, small carp waters *do* exist in the south east, as in other parts of the country, so find one if you can.

3. Tackle

Now buy your tackle, in relation to the water you are going to fish, but in the case of rods, which are expensive, bearing in mind that they should be suitable for at least your next couple of years fishing as well—until I started using the PM Carp Rod, most of my fishing was done with the same two rods which I had used for more than 10 years, and which had caught carp from one pound to 30lbs!

In your reading you will have come across much confusing advice about rods; advice which is full of technical jargon and 'fashions'. Ignore these fashions: don't buy the same type of rod that someone you know had used to catch 20's at 100 yards, or copy other people's tackle just because it is fashionable. Carp tackle fashions change rapidly, and there is no need to follow them.

Accessories. A good landing net, with knotless micro-mesh and with glass arms of not less than 30ins in length, and preferably 36ins. This is quite big enough; I've had carp of over 30lbs in my 36in net—although I do have a large one for fishing open waters containing very big fish. Industrial nylon sacks which have plenty of holes, in case you need to retain fish, where this is permitted; a weighing sling of similar material, although you can use the sack. *Recommended*: Kevin Nash 'Happy Hooker' carp sacks and weighing slings; Delkim carp sacks and weighing slings.

Tackle box or bag to your preference; I've tried boxes, Packaseats, bags, haversacks and rucksacks, and have now settled for the Terry Eustace Tackle Bag, as shown here. A rod holdall, again of your choice. The largest fishing umbrella you can get—don't skimp on this, or you will regret it in a storm: 45in diameter, and made of the 'Wave-

A good landing net is essential. Here the author displays the Kevin Maddocks
lightweight stalking net, made by Simpson's of Turnford.

Big enough for a 50! Peter with his big net; made by Mike Starkey, it has 42 inch
fibre glass arms and a huge knotless mesh.

lock' type of material which is really waterproof. Rod rests: two for each rod, of the V type, which allow the line to run unchecked through the V, if not using buzzers.

A good, comfortable chair: again I have tried just about everything you can buy, and have finally come round to what many other carp anglers had discovered before me—the folding type aluminium garden chair, which is light, easy to carry, and comfortable, although I add a 3in thick foam cushion for extra comfort. You are going to spend a lot of time sitting when you fish for carp, and a hard seat or box will soon become uncomfortable and will tend to make you lose your concentration. Arlesey Bombs, small swivels, artery forceps for removing hooks (much better than disgorgers), and you are ready to go. You will also need a good catapult, and a sharp knife.

Rods. Start with either one or two rods. If you get two you will probably want both to be of the same type, although this in itself is a fashion; I often fish with rods of different types. We don't need to go into all the jargon here, but it is likely that your easy water will not involve very long casting, and that as the fish are small you will not need heavy line. For this type of fishing you need a through-action rod—that is, one which bends all the way down to the butt. This bend absorbs the power of the fish hooked at close range, but if you get the right type it can be used for much longer casting also. Through-action rods are usually compound taper or slow taper, so this is what you need.

The test curve idea gives some indication of the power of the rod. The test curve is the amount of force necessary to bend the rod into a right angle with the butt, and a test curve of 1½ to 1¾lbs will be about right. The length depends on your taste, but the current fashion is for 11 to 12 foot rods. I would *never* use one of over 11ft, as I find them clumsy, and much of my fishing has been done with 10ft rods. A good compromise is a rod of 10ft 6ins—long enough to give some extra casting force, but still short enough to manoeuvre under trees and bushes if you fish that sort of water.

The Peter Mohan Carp Rod, featured in pictures in this book, was made for me by Veals of Bristol to be just this type of rod. It is effective at 6 or 60 yards, flexible enough for fast fish at short distance, but powerful enough to control the big ones once you start to catch them. It is built from a good quality Conoflex blank, and is black and 'modern' in appearance, with Fuji rings. I can recommend it—obviously! Two fibre glass rods, which are not too expensive, are all you need to start with and in fact rods of this type will last you many years. A word of warning—you can, of course, catch carp on all sorts of rods, but if you are going to do any serious carp fishing, it is best to buy purpose-built carp rods, and get those used by carp specialists, rather than cheap mass produced rods which may cost you less but will not really be good enough for serious carp fishing—which is why they are not used by carp specialists.

Reels. In this book I shall only recommend tackle that I use myself, or which I know is used successfully by experienced carp anglers. I have used Mitchell reels for 25 years and I feel that they are the best. Don't get a small spooled model—a mistake made by so many novices who have not read a book of this kind, but get a Mitchell 300 or 410. The new skirted spool Mitchells are also worth looking at. No reel made is perfect, but I believe that none lay the line as well, or last as long as Mitchells do, and the prices are quite reasonable. I used a 300 for 25 years, and it was still working well at the end of that time. Service and repair facilities by Leeda Tackle, the Mitchell importers, are excellent.

Line. I see many anglers using stiff, poor quality monofilament nylon line, and I suggest avoiding this. I use Milbro Maxima and another good line is Sylcast; most specialist carp anglers use one of these two lines. Bulk spools are cheaper and more convenient. Store line away from light and wet it before you tie all knots, as it is likely to lose too much of its strength if it is knotted when it is dry. It will help you to avoid breaks if you run your fingers along the last few feet of the line after each fish you catch, and cut the piece off if you feel any fraying or imperfections. 8lb line will do for most carp waters; use 10-12lb breaking strain line if the water is snaggy or heavily weeded.

Hooks. Again, there are some very poor ones about, and I am always hearing about people whose hooks break and bend etc. I have caught over 3,000 carp to 30lbs, many with heavy lines in very snaggy waters, and have never broken a hook. I use Richard Walker Carp Hooks by Bruce and Walker (B. James and Son). Au Lion d'Ors are good hooks and very popular with those who catch big carp, while some of the heavier Mustad hooks are also good (Mustad 39838, the Goldstrike, or the 39838A, the bronze version). If you use inferior brands, don't blame me if you lose fish! I would not use anything except eyed hooks, and size 4's are about right. Size 2 is also worth trying, and I can see no point for most kinds of carp fishing in using hooks smaller than English equivalent size 8 (remember that hook sizes vary). You can sharpen them if you feel that they are not sharp enough, but I have never found this to be necessary.

Bite Indicators. You need a bite indicator which is hung on the line between the reel and the butt ring, or between the first and second rings, as these are the easiest places to see them. A cylinder of white plastic is what I like best, and mine have a built-in Beta-light for night fishing. A cylinder of kitchen foil will do almost as well, but make sure it is a cylinder, and is not pinched on the line; the line must be able to run through it. Silver paper or kitchen foil can jam in the butt ring, however, so use the plastic type as soon as you can make some. I don't use electric 'buzzers' but nearly all carp anglers do, and I recommend that you should do so, although it is not essential at first. If you are not sure whether you intend to specialise in carp fishing, or if you only intend to go a few times a year, don't waste your money on them; just watch your indicators at all times, and you will catch just as many carp. However, if you start to do a lot of night fishing, if you do long sessions, or if you find your attention wanders a lot, it is worth getting them; they do often give just that bit of early warning before the indicator starts to move which will alert you and make you prepare for

Roger Emmet made these indicators for PM, although he doesn't use them himself! Peter always wanted one of this kind. Note the built-in beta-light for night fishing; this is removable to reduce weight.

The indicator clipped on the line. Peter says it has to be large, as his eyesight is not too good! A flick of the fingers will detach it from the line when a fish is hooked.

the action which is to come. *Never* use a 'buzzer' without a
bite indicator on the line, as I have seen people doing.*

* There is an exception to this statement about not using an indicator on
the line: many carp anglers in the south east now use Optonics and no
indicator on the line. This is possible because the Optonic's sound shows
how fast line is being taken; a visual indicator is not essential. However,
I still advise the use of a visible bite indicator on the line when you are
starting. The 'buzzers' I recommend are: Optonics (Dellareed); A. J. S.
(Bait '78); Heron conversions by Del Romang.

3 Tackle, Methods & Rigs

There may be people reading this book who have not done any fishing before, and who therefore need to know more about rigs and set-ups before they even start, but I hope not too many. To start with carp fishing is not really the best way to take up angling; it is better, in my opinion, that you should have done some general coarse fishing first. If you have, then the first two chapters should be enough to get you started.

Tackle . . . again

As I have already said, you can start carp fishing with almost any reasonably powerful and flexible rod, but I hope you have bought a purpose built carp rod, because it is much better, and pleasanter, to fish with the tackle for the job.

Once you have put the rod together, fix on the reel, and wind on the line. If you have a deep spool, put on some form of backing—an old line will do—because you are going to ensure that when the line is wound on, it comes to within one sixteenth of an inch (1.5mm) of the lip of the spool—slightly less for a heavy, stiff line. This is most important—the reason for many novices being unable to cast properly is that they do not have enough line on the spool so the friction when casting makes it impossible to get the bait out far, or even to get it where you want it to go. If you doubt me, go and have a look at many of the youngsters, and novice adults, who fish our waters. Their casting is bad, and their reels are loaded with line which comes half-way up the spool. I've read different ideas of how best to wind on line to avoid kinks, but I always do so by letting the line come off the side of the line spool, and in the opposite direction from the way the reel winds the line on. In other words, if your bale arm puts the line on the reel in an anti-clockwise direction, the line should be coming off the line spool *clockwise*, when you are looking at the side of the spool which is facing you, in each case. A bulk spool is useful as mentioned, because if you misjudge the amount required you can go on until the line is nearly up to the lip of the reel spool.

Put the line through the rod rings, then if you are going to freeline, just tie the hook onto the end of the line, using a five turn blood knot unless you know of a better one. Wet the line before tightening the knot, and don't cut it off too closely, in case it should slip a little.

FIVE TURN HALF BLOOD KNOT

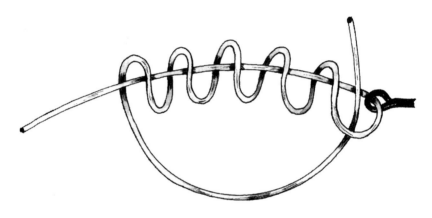

Legering

Perhaps the most popular leger rig for carp fishing, and certainly the one I use nearly all the time, is the one illustrated. The swivel acts as the line stop—I never use leger stops as they compress and may damage the line, and they often slip on hard casts.

The leger weight can be on the line, but I prefer it on a link as shown, and this is essential for soft bottomed waters, where the weight may sink up to 5 inches into the bottom. If the weight is not on a link, it will drag the line down, and may prevent it from running freely through the eye of the swivel when you have a take.

Tie one end of the line to the ring on the bomb, and 3 to 6 inches from the bomb tie a swivel to the end of the link. Then slide the other end of the swivel onto the reel line. Now tie another swivel into the end of the reel line and cut off the reel line a foot to eighteen inches (30cms to 40cms) from the swivel. You are left with a piece of line a foot to eighteen inches long, with a swivel attached to one end. Now tie the end of the reel line to the other end of the swivel, and you have a swivel tied into the reel line as an immovable stop.

STANDARD LINK LEGER RIG

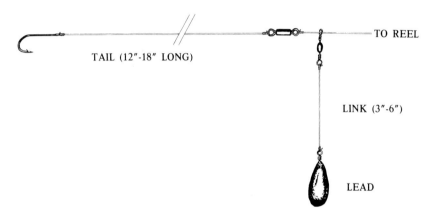

TAIL (12"-18" LONG)

TO REEL

LINK (3"-6")

LEAD

The bomb link will slide down until it rests against the swivel-stop. Now tie the hook to the other end. Use the reel line throughout—no need for 'traces' or 'bottoms' in carp fishing as all the line is usually of the same breaking strain, although you can use lighter line for the bomb link if you wish.

This is a standard leger set up, and should be adequate for all your early carp fishing, and probably most of it in the future also.

The Set-Up

I've mentioned Red Beck Lake already. This was intended to be a water where those taking up carp fishing could start off, and catch plenty of fish from the first day there, which nearly everyone does—men, women and one or two children! Those converting from other branches of angling certainly have some weird and wonderful set-ups, yet still catch carp. Some members recently were just resting the rod in the type of rod rest through which the line cannot run, and holding—all day!—the butt; no indicators. When they felt the rod tip jerk, they struck! At Red Beck, a very easy water, this works quite well, but it is unnecessarily tiring to hold the rod in this way, and you are likely to catch more carp if you use a proper carp set-up. Once the fish become more wary, they may start to eject the bait as soon as they feel resistance from the rod tip, so those using a carp set-up where resistance is minimal will catch more fish.

Put your V type rod rests in so that the rod is pointing in the direction of the bait, and also so that the rod is angled *downwards*, pointing at the bait; this minimises resistance. There is an exception to this rule, but don't bother about this at present.

Now cast—and I am not going to attempt to teach casting in this book, as it can only be demonstrated on the bank. A simple underarm or side cast will do for short distances; a double-handed overhead cast for longer distances. Sink the line by putting the rod tip under the water until it is all sunk, then place the rod in the rests. Put your bite indicator cylinder on the line between the reel and the butt ring, and pull enough line from the reel so that the line to the bomb is held tight, and the indicator just rests on the ground. In easy waters and calm weather, this is enough, but if there is any wind or drag, mount the indicator on a 'needle' as illustrated. The needle—I use the spokes of an old umbrella, but many people use welding rod—should be at an angle of 45 degrees, pointing towards the butt ring. The indicator should be exactly under the reel. Put the line round the antenna of the buzzer, or whatever else the buzzer needs to activate it, and test quickly to make sure that it isn't going to keep buzzing every time there is a bit of wind—and now you know why I don't use electric bite indicators. I got fed up with fishing waters where anglers' indicators, badly adjusted, kept buzzing at every gust of wind. One of the

The author's set-up. Note the indicators on 'needles' exactly underneath the reels.

reasons I go carp fishing is for peace and quiet, not to listen to some electronic device every few minutes. If this is a really easy water, and takes are frequent, then don't even use the buzzer—and give others a bit of peace! Or choose a quiet buzzer—one that only you can hear.

I suggest that you start with one rod only—it is all you will need in most easy waters. If you want to experiment with two different baits, or the action is not too fast, then use two rods. Set up the other alongside the first in the same way. Before casting, adjust the clutch so that line can just be pulled from the spool.

On most easy waters you will be able to fish with the bale arm OPEN; if you do, the anti-reverse should be ON, although this is not essential if you play fish by backwinding (and you will need the 'needle' to support the bite indicator). When takes are very fast, as they often are on this type of water, then an open bale arm is usually best. If takes are slower, then fish with the bale arm closed. In this case, the anti-reverse should be OFF. The reason for this is obvious, although you wouldn't think so to judge by the number of anglers I see doing this wrongly—two of whom lost rods on my Devon water because they left anti-reverses on. If the bale arm is closed, try to strike *before* the indicator reaches the rod. If you don't, some fish may drop the bait when they feel the resistance of the rod, and you will miss them. Others, however, will tear off, hooking themselves before you can strike—and the reel handle will start to spin. You should still strike, though, in case the hook has not yet penetrated past the barb. Remember—if you had the bale arm closed, and the anti-reverse ON, your reel handle could not spin, and your rod could be pulled in. I experimented with this once, on a water where the takes were very violent, and even a five pounder could pull my rod off the rests and into the water—if I left the anti-reverse on; even a tench can do it!

Now, don't retire into a 'bivvy', as you will see so many carp anglers, most of whom should know better, do, or even sit away from the rods. Sit close to the rods so that you can

Since writing the first edition of this book I have been using the KM Adjusta-level bedchair marketed by Fox International. The picture shows the bedchair set up on a steep sloping bank and I have found it perfect for all situations.

reach them without getting up from your chair. I like to be close but slightly to one side, and I recommend this, although I know that some anglers prefer to be right behind the rods. If you sit to one side, as I do, it is best to have the further rod a little higher on the rests, so that you can reach it easily over the nearer one. The height of the rods above the ground depends on you. You can have them fairly high if you are having time to stand up before the strike, but lower if you strike from a sitting position. They shouldn't be too low, or the 'drop'—the distance between the rod and the indicator—will be too small for you to strike before the indicator reaches the rod. About 18 inches (45cms) to 2ft (60cms) is about right.

There are other, more 'modern' methods of setting up the tackle and bite indicators which will be dealt with in a later chapter; here, I am only concerned with giving the beginner a set-up which is simple and which works well; that mentioned above does, and I have caught many hundreds of fish using it.

If you are freelining—which you should only do, remember, when you are fishing at very short range, with heavy baits, and on waters where the takes are very fast, the line will be slacker from the rod tip—that is, it forms a bigger bow in the water, not being straight to the bait, so the fish will have gone much further with the bait before you see any indication on the indicator, compared with legering when the line is tighter. The reason for freelining is to avoid any resistance to the take.

Now you are really carp fishing—at last. On these easy waters it probably doesn't matter much where you fish, but I will go into 'reading' the water—yes, you have to read water as well as books in the 'Mohan plan'!—and the right way to select swims, find out where the fish feed etc. in a later chapter. I wanted to get you fishing as quickly as possible, and if you really have found that easy, hungry water, the fish will take baits just about anywhere—you come to Red Beck Lake and see!

Peter telling Ron Middleton that he still prefers this type of set-up, but that he can always use the KM set-up if he doesn't like the idea of the indicators 'falling off' the end of the needles!

4 Using Your Bait

Bread. Still a very successful bait on easy waters, and for those who sneer, I caught 103 fish on freelined floating crust in the last two seasons, including 16 doubles to 15¼lb, from two of the syndicate waters I control, although I admit you're not likely to do this if you fish in the south-east of the country! Bread flake can be pinched onto the hook from a new loaf, and paste made from stalish bread mixed with water, but crust is usually best on these easy waters. In spite of being easy to fish, floating crust is used badly by most novice anglers. Often it is broken from the loaf, which makes it disintegrate easily, and a bubble float is used to aid casting. A member on one of my waters was fishing in this way recently, yet complaining to me that the carp were only

Cut the crust with a sharp knife, and leave a long 'tail' of flake . . .

'playing' with the crust, but not taking it. I explained to him that this was probably because they felt the resistance from the heavy bubble float. 'Can't cast without that', he replied. So I told him to cast as far as he could with his fractured bread and bubble float, and I then cast a freelined piece of crust nearly twice as far. 'How did you do that?', he said; so I showed him:

Take a *new* loaf, preferably of the tinned kind, and *cut* with a sharp knife, a cube of the crust from ½in (13mm) to 1½ins (38mm) square, taking care to leave a long 'tail' of flake attached to the crust. Squeeze the soft flake hard, and insert the hook as shown, so that the hook stands upright from the bait when it floats. A size four hook is best. This will remain on the hook much longer, and can be cast much further, because the crust has not been fractured by breaking. Dip the bait quickly in the water to add casting weight, and cast with a smooth swing.

. . . then squeeze the flake hard and insert the hook as shown.

This freeline crust fishing, with nothing on the line, is ideal in calm conditions and at short range. Better results seem to be achieved by ensuring that the line floats—grease it with Mucilin or Vaselene if it starts to sink—and if takes are frequent, hold the rod all the time. If things are slow, put it in the rests with an indicator in the usual way. Don't strike at the first swirl at the crust—even if it disappears—as the fish often hold the crust in the protractile lips for a while and an early strike will pull the bait from their mouths. At the first sign of activity in the region of the bait, drop your eyes to the line, and don't strike until it tightens to the rod, or until the indicator is going. This is a very effective method at night also, and again I hold the rod all the time unless takes are few. Whenever I fish in this way—a bit of a speciality of mine—I drape the line over the fingers as shown, which enables me to feel the first movement of the line. I also use this method for very short range stalking with freelined light baits, and almost never miss a take. It's like 'touch' legering, I suppose, but without the leger. Do not fish like this except at *very* short range, or you may suffer from 'bite-offs'.

Hold the rod all the time for short range stalking; you can feel the fish pick up the bait if the line is held over the fingers.

Anchored floating crust. For fishing at longer distances, or in windy conditions, the anchored crust method is best. There are different rigs, but I use the one illustrated. This time you can use slightly staler bread with less flake, so that it is more buoyant. Hook the crust from the other side, so that the hook projects downwards. The corners of the loaf are very buoyant, so try these if you have difficulty in getting the bait to come up in deep water. After casting, slacken the line and wait for the crust to reach the surface—you should see it bob up, though you might need binoculars at long range. When it is floating, tighten the line so that the slightest pull will make the crust go under, then put the rod on the

ANCHORED CRUST OR FLOATER RIG

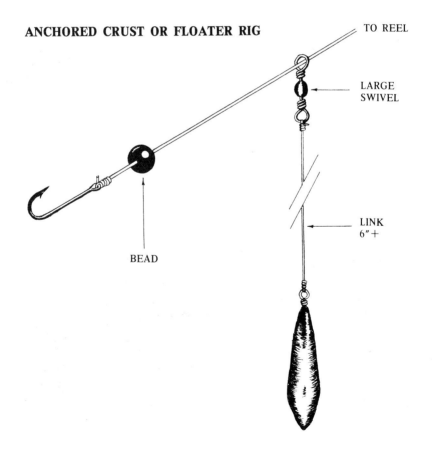

TO REEL

LARGE
SWIVEL

LINK
6″ +

BEAD

rests with an indicator in the usual way. This method has the advantage that the crust can easily be pulled just under the water to defeat the attentions of water birds. Try not to hook water birds when using floating baits, as it gets anglers a bad name with those who have prejudices against angling, and never kill them.

Legered crust. Fished on a standard leger method, with the hook link from 4ins (10cms) to 15ins (38cms), crust is often a deadly bait on easy waters, and even on some more difficult ones, as it rises in the water, is easily visible and attracts fish by its movement as they pass close by.

LEGERED CRUST OR FLOATER RIG

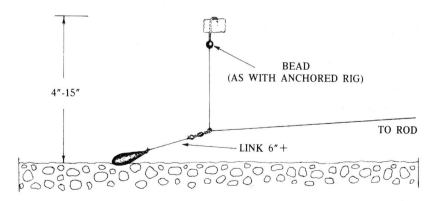

BEAD
(AS WITH ANCHORED RIG)

4"-15"

TO ROD

LINK 6"+

Sunk freelined crust. It is possible to make crust sink and to fish it freeline by squeezing the air out of the crust under water after it is put on the hook. The crust, cast gently, will sink slowly and may be taken 'on the drop', or soon after it reaches the bottom. An excellent method for close range fishing in deep water, I have called this method for years my 'secret' bait, as I have caught plenty of good carp with it, often very quickly, and even alongside good high protein baits which have remained untouched for several hours!

I hope the details on bread fishing will convince the reader that there are still many waters where carp can be caught by this bait and with simple methods. To prove this to myself, while writing this chapter I went to fish two of my 'easy' waters, using *exactly* the methods and baits listed above. I used one rod, holding it all the time as shown. On one water I had 11 carp, best 10.2, in 2 hours; on the second, I had 8 in 4 hours, all between 6 and 10½lbs, and great fun it was, I can assure you, with all the fish going off at great speed against 8lb line and a light rod. So don't despise floating crust; at the right time on the right water it will outfish the best HP bait ever devised—I've proved this many times!

Luncheon meat. Most types of tinned luncheon meat work well, cut into cubes of from ½in (13mm) to one inch (25mm). Some of the biggest carp ever taken in this country were caught on this bait, and every season carp anglers are catching 20's and 30's, often from quite hard waters on this bait, while others are spending much time on more exotic concoctions. Fish a leger rig and throw in 6-10 pieces of the meat around each hook bait before starting. Pre-baiting is not needed. Bacon Grill is a particularly good luncheon meat. Luncheon meat is a very good winter bait on many waters.

Sausage meat. Sausage meat can be made into a good bait when stiffened with breadcrumbs, flour, or perhaps best of all, a proprietary ground bait.

Pet foods. Most tinned pet food such as Kit-E-Kat can also be made into very good baits. Don't add any water, but simply stiffen with breadcrumbs, ground bait or flour. Make sure it is made stiffly enough so that it doesn't break up in water. Once stiffened, you can make yet another good bait by using 50 per cent of pet food paste mixed with 50 per cent sausage meat. If you have difficulty in hooking fish, leave the point and bend of the hook protruding from the bait. Again throw or catapult a few free offerings round each hook bait. Pre-baiting is often not needed on these easy waters, but if the action is slow, put in 50 or so baits when you leave, or even before you start, although this should only be done when no-one else is fishing near, for obvious reasons. In one easy water I once fished with a friend, we put in 80 baits of this kind before starting, and I had a carp within half an hour!

Pastes can also be made from the hard type pet foods such as Munchies and Go-Cat, by soaking the pieces in water or by grinding to a powder, and then mixing to a paste with stiffening.

Trout pellet paste. Along with pet food baits, TP can be classed as a bait with a medium protein content—bread and sweet corn are fairly low in protein value. Trout pellets can be obtained from a fish farm, where they are much cheaper when bought in large bags, or as 'Pond Pride' and other brand names from shops which sell food for aquarium fish and goldfish ponds, and also from the bait suppliers mentioned in this book. Possibly the best way is to grind the pellets to a powder and then mix into a paste, but I am always in favour of doing things the easiest way, and I have always mixed mine by simply pouring boiling water onto the pellets—one third of a pint of water to a pint of trout pellets is usually about right. Allow to cool, then knead to a paste. Some of the modern TP tends to crumble in water, and may need stiffening as with other baits. There is no need to add anything else, as this is a complete fish food, with a strong smell. Some pre-baiting may be necessary, though on easy waters I would expect that no more than 100-200 baits would be needed to get the fish going. Be warned, however—tench and other species love this bait.

BALANCED HOOKBAIT

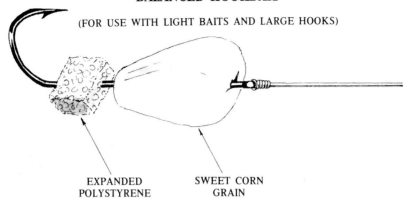

(FOR USE WITH LIGHT BAITS AND LARGE HOOKS)

EXPANDED   SWEET CORN
POLYSTYRENE   GRAIN

Sweet Corn. Your first multiple bait, sometimes called 'particle' baits by carp anglers. Sweet corn, straight from the tin, seems to attract fish very quickly, so no pre-baiting is needed. Just throw in a handful, and fish amongst it. A catapult will get the grains out further, but it is not easy to get the baits out a long way. Put 2-6 grains on a size 4 or 6 hook. Do not attempt to hide the hook—it is not necessary. Eventually, the carp may become wary of more than one piece on the hook, and you may have to use a single piece. Most other species are very fond of this bait also.

I would suggest that you should not try to take short cuts, and in most easy or fairly easy waters this will not be necessary. There is nothing magical in HP baits, although many beginners seem to think so. They are far more trouble to prepare, and on the sort of waters I have been advising, they will not catch any more carp than the baits I have listed in this chapter; they may, in fact, catch less, as it is often much harder to get them going on the more 'advanced' baits.

Persist with a bait, even if it is not working at first; don't give up too easily. This is where two rods can be useful—try a second bait on the other rod. Vary bait sizes if things are slow, and cast to other areas.

5 Striking, Hooking, Playing, Landing & Looking After Your Carp

Striking

Takes vary so much that it is impossible to teach anyone how and when to strike, but there are a few useful indications. When fishing with an open bale arm, make the strike as soon as the indicator is moving; you will be fishing for fast takes, and the line will probably be peeling from the spool by the time you react, so strike as soon as you can. Grab the rod and at the same time turn the reel handle with the other hand to engage the pick up and sweep it back hard. Before you start, make sure that the clutch is adjusted so that line can be pulled from the spool when you hook the fish, as in this type of fishing your anti-reverse will be closed, and you may get broken on the strike unless the clutch can give line. I have mine looser than most people.

If you are fishing with the bale arm closed, you will be fishing for shorter, slower takes (though you may get the fast one anyway, when the reel handle will spin). Try to strike before the indicator reaches the rod, preferably just before. Strike hard, with an upward sweep unless there are overhead trees, when you will have to strike sideways. Some carp anglers advocate a sideways strike anyway, and I find that my own strike is somewhere in between an overhead and a side strike. At long range (60 yards plus) I think the strike should always be a big overhead sweep, with the rod as vertical as possible. At very close range, the strike can be less hard.

Types of take. In general, most carp takes can be divided into three categories: *screamers*, when the take is very fast, with the indicator rattling in the butt ring, and the line being torn off the spool. You should never miss these, but don't

About to strike . . . you may prefer to stand up, but in this case there wasn't time.

panic, or you may do so; *feeding takes*, when the indicator goes up quite slowly, but sometimes in jerks, to the rod, which you should strike just before the indicator touches the rod; and *twitchers*, which take in short jerks. On your easy waters you are likely to get only the first two categories.

Many so-called 'twitches' on these waters are line bites or other species interfering with the bait. Last season I watched a fairly inexperienced carp angler on one of my waters strike every few minutes at twitches, and miss every one. This is a heavily stocked water with fish often touching the line, while small fish often jerk at the bait. All the carp takes are good fast runs, so I told him to ignore all movements of the indicator, even if it went a couple of feet, but to open the bale arm and strike only the fast runs. This worked, and he caught several carp.

There *is* a twitcher problem on some more difficult waters, which I will deal with later.

Reasons for missing takes

Striking too soon (rare on easy waters, although common with floating baits); striking too late, often because of slow reactions by the angler; not striking hard enough; bait too stiff (leave the point and bend of the hook exposed when using hard or stiff baits); bait too large, when it is often carried by small carp in the protractile lips, and the strike will pull the bait from the mouth (obvious remedy is to reduce the bait size, or use a larger hook); panicking by the angler, often watching paralysed as the line tears off the spool, or alternatively leaping from the chair, knocking the rod and rests over, and not getting the strike right; not using a proper bite indication system—if the carp can feel the resistance of the rod tip, or any other strong resistance they may eject the bait before you can make the strike; using blunt hooks; using too small hooks which do not take hold properly.

Playing fish

This is very easy in an open water with no snags, but at all times you should keep a steady strain on the fish, with the rod well up when the fish is a long way away from you, and the rod point lower when the fish is near. Don't 'pump', even at long range, as constantly lowering and raising the rod, and allowing the line to go slack, during this silly technique, once much favoured by big fish anglers, tends to loosen the hook hold.

If there is adjacent weed or snags, you will need to *think* when playing the fish, and your tactics for most eventualities should have been worked out in advance, before a fish is hooked. If the fish goes hard for a nearby snag, sidestrain may turn it, so lower the rod to one side of you until it is parallel with the water, and hold the fish. Be prepared to move your position, something which I rarely see carp anglers doing, but which may prevent you losing a fish. Move to get into a better position to keep the fish away from snags, move backwards, if possible, especially when fishing at long range, if the line goes slack and the fish appears to be swimming towards you; walk sideways, pulling the fish

Playing a fish; landing net at the ready.

with you to get it away from snags—the carp often follows.

There are two methods of playing big fish—using the clutch which you adjust constantly according to the amount of pull exercised by the fish; and backwinding, in which the clutch is kept tight, and the anti-reverse is *off*, allowing the handle to turn backwards when the fish takes line. Backwinding is now popular with carp anglers, mainly because many think that it is the best way to control big fish. I am not sure this is so, and my own playing is a mixture of both methods, although I do like to hear that clutch scream! If using the backwinding method, watch for a very fast run, when a flying handle can do you a lot of damage if it catches any part of your body, while you may get broken if you obstruct the free turning of the handle.

Reasons for losing fish when playing them

Clutch too tight—fish break line; holding fish too hard—line is broken; using too light line. (NB. Most breaks are the fault of the angler; you have done something wrong—your line is too light; it is old and has weak points; you tried to hold the fish too hard, and actually 'pulled out', pulling the hook through the flesh of the fish. A too stiff, too powerful rod can also cause this, which is why I do not recommend the use of fast taper rods for beginners. *Never* accept breaks; they are not bad luck, but bad angling, and they are rarely the fault of the tackle, but of the angler. If you get broken, work out the reason, and don't let it happen again. It should be very rare, and if it is frequent you are fishing badly, and you should *stop* before you damage more fish, and work out the reasons before you start again. I often get letters from people who claim to get broken frequently—they should stop fishing until they can cure this, and I would ban them on my own waters. It is far better to get fewer takes using heavier line than to use light lines and get broken. Don't be afraid of heavy line; top carp anglers have caught very big carp on line up to 25lbs BS, in circumstances where it was needed, but as a general rule I would say that if you are still getting breaks on good, new 15lbs BS line, because of weed or snags, you should give up fishing in that area.)

Letting the line go slack, when the hook slips out; hook not taking hold properly — you need a larger hook (or possibly a smaller one when fishing at very long range), a sharper hook, or to have more of the hook exposed in a hard bait; panicking; letting the fish get into weed and snags. If you cannot keep it out—and only experience will tell you how hard you can hold fish without either getting broken, or pulling out, which is another reason for spending a season catching plenty of small fish, and learning how to play them —keep a steady strain on the line, and you may be able to pull the fish out by the way it went in. This especially applies to lilies and other loose weed. If this doesn't work, careful handlining, after putting the rod down, may get the fish to move out. As a last resort, slacken off, and be prepared to wait for 5 to 10 minutes for the fish to free itself. This is often recommended, but in my experience it rarely works and is very much a last resort. Remember to check the last few yards of your line for weaknesses each time you are snagged or weeded.

You may also lose fish when they are accidentally foul hooked, when the scale or flesh gives and they often come off.

Landing

In your first year, land *all* your fish yourself, as you need this experience. Even after this, try to land as many as you can, and *never* let a stranger net your fish—he may not do it properly, and may lose you a good fish; it once happened to me! If a stranger picks up your net, ask him politely to put it down, and explain this by saying that you like to net all your fish yourself. You needn't tell him he's useless, even though he may be! Later, you may welcome the help of a trusted friend, especially at night or in difficult circumstances.

Wait until the fish looks played out, then lower the net into the water, and bring the fish over the net. *Never* chase it with the net, or you may catch, and break, the line. When the fish is well over the net, lift until it is engulfed, then slide the hand up to the spreader block, and lift. With a big fish, you may need to put down the rod and lift the mesh of

Netting sequence. Bring the fish over the net, which is held, without moving, in the water . . .

... wait until the head of the carp is well towards the spreader block ...

... then lift.

If the fish is big, don't lift from the end of the net handle, or it may break. Lift the spreader block with one hand, while the other gathers and lifts the mesh.

the net with the other hand, to avoid putting too much strain on the net handle, which could break. Make sure you have a big enough net, or you may lose your best fish ever when you can't get it into the net.

Unhooking

Place the fish on soft ground if possible, and cover with a wet sack or something similar if it thrashes about a lot. If the hook doesn't come out easily, try to avoid damaging the mouth by threading the eye of the hook through the flesh, and cutting the line. If the hook is well down, use the artery forceps to extract it. Remember that the less damage you can do to the mouth the better condition it will be in for the future.

Retaining fish

Don't keep the fish out of the water for more than three or four minutes, and try to return it at once. If you need to keep it, put it in a large carp sack made of industrial nylon with

If possible, thread the hook through rather than tear it out against the barb, and cut it off as shown. Little damage to the mouth will occur if unhooking is done this way.

holes, or mesh curtain net material. Do *not* use a keep net, or even a mesh-netting, so-called 'carp sack', as the netting damages the fish. The correct type of sack is dark, and the fish, unable to see freedom, as it can in a net, will not thrash about. Put in deep water, preferably in shade, and check regularly to see that all is well. Never keep for more than a few hours, and return the fish at once if it shows any sign of distress.

When returning carp, lower them gently into the water, and support the fish until it swims off. If it starts to keel over, continue to hold it until it recovers its balance.

Photographing

Do not take long, and hold the fish with wet hands. Keep it as low as possible, preferably over water or soft ground. A finger or two in the mouth gives a better hold. Support the stomach if it is fat or carrying spawn. Pour water on the gills after 3 or 4 minutes; return to the water frequently for a brief spell if you are indulging in a protracted photographic session. Cover the fish with a wet sack while it is lying on the ground, as this often prevents the fish from struggling. Treat **all** carp as carefully as I have recommended, even if they are small fish. I have no time for those who regard small carp with contempt and who therefore treat them carelessly. The little three pounder may live for 30 years, may reach 20 to 30lbs, and give much pleasure to many anglers in the future.

BCSG/SW Regional Organiser Roger Emmet, from Tewkesbury, Gloucs., with one of his 90 doubles, caught in less than two years from local waters. This one, a fine linear mirror, weighed 20lb 14oz.

18.4: summer 1982.

6 Night Fishing

Those who are taking up carp fishing often appear to believe that a combination of HP baits, expensive 'buzzers', and night fishing is the recipe for instant success as a carp angler. I hope that I have already shown that the first two are not essential, and it is not necessary to fish after dark either, at least on some of the easy carp waters I know. Some waters fish best during the day, but other easy waters may well be better after dark.

However, if you are going to do any night fishing, it is best to learn to do it properly from scratch. First of all, if you are nervous fishing after dark, to the extent that you need company, noise and lights, then it is better that you should not go night fishing at all. Even if noise and light don't disturb the carp, and often they do not, you will disturb other anglers who enjoy the peace and quiet of night fishing.

To try it out, start by fishing an evening and continuing for a couple of hours after dark, and see how you get on. Before it gets dark and while you can still see, do the following:

1. Throw in a few more free offerings in the areas in which you are going to fish;

2. Bring in your baits, make sure the end tackle is in good condition, re-bait and recast, making sure you get them amongst the free offerings;

3. Look carefully at trees, bushes or other markers on the skyline, and watch these as it gets dark; this will give you something to aim at at night;

4. Make sure your set-ups are right, that the rods are easy to reach from your seat or bedchair, and that you are going to be able to see the indicators; betalights are useful here;

5. Arrange your tackle tidily so that you can put your hand on all objects you are likely to need, especially the bait, in the darkness;

6. Place the landing net so that you can find it easily;
7. Put a torch where you can find it, but make up your mind *not* to use it, except in an emergency.
8. Make sure you are comfortable, that you have plenty of room, and that you know exactly where any snags or weed beds are placed, and that you know just where any overhead branches or bushes are. Choose open swims as far as possible for your first night fishing attempts.
9. Rehearse what you are going to do when a fish is hooked.
10. Make up your mind that you will go at a certain time, unless catches are very good, or before if you start to lose your alertness.

Few nights are really dark, and as the light goes you may well be surprised at what you can still see. Make up your mind to learn to do *everything* without using a torch; the light may not worry the fish, although sometimes it does,

This linear mirror weighed 23¼lbs. The author is seen here holding it after catching it on a paste bait at midnight, in June 1981.

but each time you put on a light you will lose some of your night vision, and this takes some time to re-establish. Casting, putting on the bait, playing and landing the fish can all be done in the dark easily, once you have practised. Some people can even tie a hook in the dark, and this can certainly be done by holding the hook up against any light there is, or even against the moon. The torch is for emergencies only. If you get into a tangle, or find there is something you cannot do without light, then take the torch well away from the waterside to do what you have to. As I have said, even if the light doesn't affect the fish, then waving torches at the waterside will certainly upset other carp anglers who, like myself, find it most irritating to night fish a water near people using lights.

I would sooner use a torch to net a big fish at night, than lose it, but even here the light will destroy your night vision, and it is better to learn to land the fish in complete darkness.

When casting, listen carefully to the splash when the bait lands, and try to judge the amount of time the baits spend in flight; as you gain experience, you will find you can cast more accurately to the right area in the dark than you might think, aided by your silhouetted markers still visible against the skyline, and the splash of the lead landing, combined with the length of time the bait is in flight. When a fish is hooked, crouch and watch the bend of the rod against the sky, which should give you some idea of which way the fish is going. Play it out well, and try to pull the head of the fish right over the net up to the spreader block before you lift. Freelined floating crust or floater fishing at night is great fun and often very effective, even on waters where this bait is not taken during the day. If you are freelining in this way, reel in until the hook clicks into the tip ring; you then know where it is, which is better than having it swinging around, and perhaps hooking yourself.

Baits and methods are the same as in the day time, and you will usually find the fish in the same areas, especially if you have been putting baits into an area during the day. When you pack up, and in fact at all times, be even quieter than usual to avoid upsetting anyone else who is still fishing, and don't throw in lots of baits before you leave if there are others fishing the lake.

I have seen all sorts of peculiar bite indication systems used at night, from the chap who told me he never used a torch at night, only a candle in a jar to illuminate his indicator, to the angler who held the rod on his knee all the time, striking whenever he 'felt' anything! A quiet buzzer to give you an early warning, or the usual indicator with a beta-light built in, is all you need for night fishing.

Have plenty of warm clothes; most summer nights are surprisingly cold, and you will not fish well unless you are comfortable. If you find yourself nodding off, then waking with a start at the sound of the buzzer, and missing the fish on the strike, then pack up and go home; you are not fishing efficiently, and are better off waiting until another day.

If your short spell of night fishing proves productive, and you feel it is worth staying all night, perhaps to be in position for first light, which is a good time on some waters, then make sure you have even more warm and waterproof clothes, a comfortable chair, probably a bed chair, and plenty of food and drink. Use a big umbrella if it is cold, wet or windy, but be careful to position it so that you can strike easily without the rod hitting the umbrella, even if this means you must fish a bit further from your rods. Do *not* use a tent or 'bivvy'; you will miss a lot of fish if you do. Don't strike at the first 'buzz'; watch your indicator and strike when it acts in the same way as it does in the day time.

Keep notes of the time the fish are caught, the weather, and the light—some waters fish better in 'bad' weather, or when it is cloudy; a few fish best on moonlit nights. Above all, don't waste your time night fishing *unless* it proves much more productive than in the day time, and unless you do it simply because you enjoy the extra peace and quiet of night time fishing—or you want to get away from the wife!

7 Winter Carp Fishing

Unless you have become so keen that you can't keep away from the water, my advice to beginners on winter carp fishing is . . . don't! It is mostly very hard, with long cold blanks, and many of them, except on a few freak waters, where the fishing can be as good as in the summer. However, if, like me, you simply must go carp fishing, then a couple of winter carp trips a week may well be worth doing, especially if your water fishes well in the winter. I do almost as much carp fishing in the winter as I do in the summer, and have done so for 30 years; but then, I don't like heat, so the cold weather worries me very little.

The following points are worth noting for those who want to carry on after November 1st, the normal start of winter carp fishing:

1. Find a water where carp do take baits in the winter—your easy, overstocked water may well be one, but not all easy waters fish well in the winter.

2. Fish short sessions, and try to find out the best time, fishing these only and staying at home during the barren periods;

3. Do more in long mild spells, less in frosty weather;

4. Fish during the dark of the evening—most winter waters I know fish best from 6pm till midnight, though a few go well from midday to mid-afternoon. Waters vary a lot in this respect, so find out the best time;

5. Unless you have evidence to suggest otherwise, fish the same area as in the summer, although on some waters—but not all—deeper areas are better. I have caught winter carp at depths of down to 27ft, but I've also had carp on floating crust in every month of the year, including nights when there is ice on the water!;

6. Remember that most experienced winter carp anglers

have found that mildish, overcast nights are best in the winter, with clear frosty nights the least productive;

7. Takes may be slower and shorter in the winter. You may even have to strike short twitches, which will produce big fish, which means closed bale arms, short drops, and quick strikes;

8. Use the same baits as usual, but if results are poor, smaller baits might be worth trying, and slightly lighter lines if you are fishing open water (but not less than 6lbs BS, I suggest);

9. Don't be put off by the cold, blank appearance of the water, or those who tell you that winter carp fishing is a waste of time. If you want to do it enough, then keep trying. To give you some confidence, I can reveal that many thousands of winter carp are caught each season, even in January and February; hundreds of winter 20's and quite a few winter 30's have been taken by specialist carp anglers, but these winter catches are rarely reported in the papers, for obvious reasons. Kevin Maddocks once had 84 winter doubles in a season, ten of which were 20's!;

10. Get very warm clothes—a one-piece lined suit, with warm underwear and at least one jacket under it, is best, with thick trousers and the insulated 'snow boots' now so popular, and which have transformed winter fishing for most of us. Never let yourself get too cold, as you will be inefficient, and I have even read of anglers having suffered from exposure through winter night fishing in inadequate clothes. Take plenty of hot drinks, warm coverings if you use a bed chair, and place your umbrella—I don't advocate 'bivvies' even for winter fishing—so that it protects you from the wind, and reduces the so called 'wind chill factor', which makes you even colder.

I infuriate my friends by pacing up and down rapidly every hour or so to get warm, though I had to stop this once, when close range winter fishing on one water, where my friend Roger Emmet was able to prove to me that my pacing up and down was actually preventing the fish from taking baits—his baits, of course; I was too cold to care!

Alternative set-up sometimes used by the author in windy conditions.

If you are catching nothing, and you are really cold, bored and miserable—go home. Remember, you are fishing for enjoyment, not only for 'results'. There is, however, an immense satisfaction in landing a good carp in very cold winter weather, especially with frost and snow on the ground. I once had an 11 pounder actually *under* ice, which had been spreading over the water since I cast; the fish broke thin ice twice while being played—with the rod tip under the water to prevent an ice edge from cutting it—and this on a difficult water, even in the summer.

I control one water which never freezes, being spring and stream fed, and down which you could almost trot a float in the winter, and this has proved a very good winter water, with fish up to nearly 20lbs being caught often. Another good winter water is a very deep quarry, so look for this type of water if your usual ones don't fish well in the winter.

Finally, I have to say that location is often all in winter—find the 'hotspot'—in the cold water!—and you may get quite a few fish, whilst a few yards away there will not even be a touch. Finding the fish is difficult, though, and it is impossible to draw up any rules—each water is different. Having tried all the obvious places — summer swims, remains of weed, near snags and in deep water, then you will just have to keep moving until you find them. I suspect that many winter failures are because the fish have not been located, and that they can be caught on most waters once they are found.

Waters that receive some bait on a regular basis generally produce better, especially 'hungry' waters.

8 Reading a Water

It may surprise some readers that I have left this chapter, and the next, to so late in the book, but I believe them to be less important when you are starting carp fishing, although you should find some of this information useful in the future.

In the easy waters, carp can often be caught almost anywhere, but those who can get to know a water better may have the edge on others.

Faced by a new water, it is not always easy to know where to start fishing, and for this reason many anglers start in the nearest, or the most convenient, swim. This is often the worst place to fish, as these areas must get fished more heavily, and eventually the fish may start to avoid them. Look for the less accessible places, which are least fished, even if they are a bit more inconvenient, and try them if the usual swims are not producing fish. Walk round the lake and look for features, such as weed, lily and reed beds; fallen trees or snags; the margins of islands; stream inlets, and any other feature which might attract the fish. Try one of these, remembering to use heavy lines of 12-15lbs breaking strain if fishing very near any kind of snag. Carp often feed in very shallow water, especially in warm weather, so when walking round, look for fish in the water, or swirls or fish leaping, which show where they may be. Smokescreening— clouds of mud from feeding fish stirring the bottom, or bubbles, may indicate areas to fish. Leaping fish are sometimes not feeding, but they may be.

It is not a bad idea to make a plan of the water, and also to try to get some idea of what the bottom is like. This is best done from a boat, but plumbing can also help. If the water contains bars or ridges, such as are often found in gravel pits, then both the tops of the bars, and the troughs, may be good feeding areas. If the troughs are heavily weeded, but the tops of the bars are clear, it may well be possible to get the fish to feed in the clear, shallow bar tops by putting some baits on them.

In quarries, there are often ledges and galleries which are worth fishing once you know where they are, and deeper holes in shallow waters may be worth trying.

The weather may often help you to find fish. It is usually said that especially on large open waters, fish are most likely to be found on the windward side, and when in doubt it is worth fishing into the wind, and quite close in, to see if the fish are there. This does not always work, however, and you may do best with the wind behind you—it all depends on the water. On one of my small waters, a dammed lake with the central area about 10 feet deep, it is almost impossible to catch carp in the central area. In fact, more than 75 per cent of the water seems to produce no takes at all. You have to be within a couple of feet of the lily beds, the edges of the reeds, or the island, to get any takes at all, and you can imagine how difficult it is to cast to these areas accurately, especially after dark.

Try to learn as much about the water as you can, so that finding the areas where the carp will take baits is easier. The instinct of beginners is often to cast as far into the middle as they can, where they may well catch nothing, while the fish are feeding only a couple of rod lengths out. This particularly applies in waters which shelve very steeply; you may well get most fish almost under the rod tip. This is why you need to know something about the depths of the water, and the features on the bottom.

By all means fish your favourite swim, perhaps the one which is most comfortable, or nearest the car. However, once you are not catching much here, be prepared to move, if possible, to another area, such as one of those already mentioned. Note where others catch, too; it might be useful to you on your next trip.

Stalking

Learning to 'read' the water, and to find out where the fish are likely to be, is particularly relevant to stalking carp,

Peter Mohan stalks a good carp using a floater. Look carefully and you can see the fish
swirling at the bait in the centre of the picture. Shortly after this,
a common of 19.2 was landed . . .

a method of fishing which I have not mentioned so far
because it is much easier for beginners to fish statically at
first. Anyway, stalking is not necessary on the easy waters,
although once the fish start to take less often, it may produce
some extra fish which you would not have caught by sitting
still. Obviously, you cannot do much stalking on a crowded
water; you may be unpopular if you start disturbing others
by wandering around the bank.

However, if the water is quiet, go off to look for fish with a
single rod, a net, and the minimum of tackle. In hot weather,
carp will lie in or near weed or snags, and you should be able
to catch them with floating crust or other floating baits
mentioned later. If they are on the surface in this way, you
will be able to see them. Although these carp are not
feeding, they will often take a floating bait if you can get it
near them without any disturbance. Try to position the bait
as near as you can to the mouth, for in hot weather the fish
will often not move far for a bait. Hold the rod at all times,

and strike as soon as you are sure that the bait has been taken.

If you see fish moving about slowly, or, in more opaque water, swirls or water movements indicating that the fish are moving slowly, a normal bottom bait, usually fished freeline, and cast a few feet in front of the fish, will often be picked up quite quickly. Hold the rod, and strike when you see the line moving off. If the fish are moving quickly they are 'travelling', and are not often caught. You will need to be very quiet and still for this type of fishing. Most of the time you should keep out of sight of the fish if you can, but if there is no cover, stand or crouch quite still, and the fish will often take the bait while you are in plain view, as long as you make no sudden movement. I have caught double figure carp, clearly visible under the rod tip, when they must have been able to see me, but were not alarmed because I stood still. The lower down you get, the less likely the fish are to be able to see you, as their line of sight makes it hard to see those objects which are near to the ground. We are now using hard, boiled baits for stalking and Roger, who rather specialises in this type of fishing, frequently gets doubles under the rod tip in weed which take the 'boilies' *literally* within 30 seconds of them going in!

In fact, I suggest remaining as much out of sight as possible, and as quiet as you can, when indulging in all methods of carp fishing; your clothes should be dark colours such as green or brown, too. While in some of the easy waters you can catch carp while sitting up in full view of the fish wearing a white shirt, on others they will undoubtedly see you, and will move away. Remember that fish can see through water which you find opaque, so they may well see you before you see them. This is important when stalking.

This is an especially enjoyable method of fishing when you are alone on a small, clear water, when you can move slowly round the lake, fishing whenever a fish is spotted. I've caught a lot of carp in this way. Needless to say, on many of the big, heavily fished waters, fish simply are not often seen in this way, and stalking is impossible. It often surprises me how little some carp anglers know about the waters they fish. Some have no idea of the varying water depths, and have never found out about 'holding areas' where there are always carp, even if they won't always take the baits there. Big fish often find these holding areas right under the bank, and spend much time in these areas, which is why they are not often seen. Find this place, and you may well catch a big fish in a place where you would not have expected one to be. Don't thump about on the bank, though; carp may not worry much about sound, or may not even hear it—though I prefer to keep as quiet as possible, as human speech is well within the range of a carp's hearing, according to the scientists—but they can detect vibration through the water caused by you thumping about on the bank, and this may well drive them out of the area.

Having said this, carp are very curious creatures, and when we were once building a bridge on a water, and hammering huge pegs into the ground, a shoal of carp up to 20lbs swam about a few feet out, obviously to see what the noise was about! This is not much help to the angler, though, as they certainly wouldn't have taken a bait.

The angler who knows his own water and its features, and the habits of the carp in that water, is already one up on those who don't, and it will help him a lot, especially when the fish get more difficult to catch or at times when takes are slow.

The author caught these two fish within 3 hours of each other one evening in the
'82-'83 season. Weights: 20.4 and 18.6.

9 Some Facts About Carp

It is not necessary to have most of the information in this chapter, which is why I have left it for later in the book, but all these facts are interesting, and some may help with your fishing.

I don't think the biology of the carp is relevant in a book of this kind, but I am again surprised by how little some anglers seem to know about the fish they spend so much time trying to catch, so I'll give some facts here.

The Latin name for the carp is Cyprinus Carpio, and apart from crucians which are a separate species, mirrors, commons and leathers are but *varieties* of the same species, which is why they have the same Latin name.

In fact, in the wild the carp, which comes from Central Asia, is always a common carp. In the last century, biologists in Germany wanted to breed carp for the table, as they are highly regarded as food in Europe and in Israel. By means of selective breeding, they produced carp with fewer scales, and which had a faster growth rate. These were the first mirrors and leathers which we know. The result of these experiments are often called king carp; so today we have their descendants, which are king common carp, king mirror carp, and king leather carp. To make matters more complicated, there are three distinct types of mirror carp: *scattered* mirrors, with the scales irregularly placed; *linear* mirrors, which have a clearly defined, unbroken line of scales along the lateral line, as well as a few other scales; and *fully scaled* mirrors, which look a bit like commons, but with larger scales all over. The true *leather* has only a few scales along the dorsal fin and at the tail or no scales at all (see Jim Gregory's article in the First BCSG Book). Most of our waters are stocked today with these king carp.

The original wild carp are all commons, of course, and there are very few waters left which contain genuine wild carp, although often even experienced carp anglers talk of catching 'wildies' from waters full of mirrors! In fact, you can only say that a carp is a wild carp if you can *prove* that no king carp have ever been stocked in the water, or if you know that king carp have been put into the water but have never bred. Once the carp start to spawn, the wild carp spawn gets mixed with the king carp spawn, and the fish which hatch, although they may turn out to be long, thin commons, are not true wild carp. To be on the safe side, never call a common a wildie—unless you can prove that it is!

This is a complex subject, about which I could go into much greater detail which would not be appropriate in a book of this kind. For instance, as the years go by, each spawning, in most cases, produces each year a greater proportion of common carp, until a water stocked *only* with mirrors can contain eventually nothing but commons, but this can take many years. Confused—ah well, I only mentioned this here because I wanted to stop people claiming any long thin commons they catch as wild carp!

Wild carp are said to live about 25 years, but king carp are well known to live for over thirty years, and as much as 40; no-one knows the exact life span of these fish.

The average growth rate for the country is about one pound a year, and they grow for about 15 years, though may continue to put on weight up to 20 years, and sometimes even later. Once they have reached their maximum, they maintain it, though in their later years they may well lose weight—'going back', it is called—and this is also well documented. In rich waters carp may grow at 2 to 3lbs a year, and exceptionally even more than this, although such growth rates may not be maintained for many years in succession.

Water temperatures need to reach the upper 60's °F if the carp are to spawn—remember they are not a fish native to this country, but come from warmer waters. I estimate that carp never spawn at all, or at least no young hatch, in about half of the carp waters I know, either through the water temperature not being high enough, or because the carp are barren. Spawning day on a carp water is quite a sight, with the fish thrashing about amid huge clouds of spray, oblivious to all else; try to get to observe it once, if you have never seen it; you won't forget it in a hurry.

Carp can extend the 'telescopic'—the correct word is protractile—lips for quite a way, and withdraw them to suck in baits from at least 6 inches away, even on the bottom. It is this movement of the lips that makes the distinctive 'cloop' at surface baits.

The nerve endings on the lateral line are very sensitive to vibration (your feet on the bank!), and the mucus which covers the scales is a protection against disease, so try not to remove too much of it when the fish is out of the water, by making sure that everything which touches the fish is first wetted.

Scale reading on carp is generally a waste of time. The scales are very hard to read, and biologists can usually only say that the fish is '8 years +', or something similar. Do not remove scales from carp for scale reading; it does not do the fish much good, and, as I have said, it is largely a waste of time. The only sure way to age a carp is to kill it and have an expert examine the opercular bone—don't do this either, but put *every* carp back, however large or small.

Some carp develop sores for various reasons, and it won't hurt them, and might even help, if you dab on some tincture of iodine or acriflavine which can be obtained from any chemist. Carp diseases are hard to treat and Water Authorities should be notified if a disease is suspected. If you think it might be an infectious disease, inform the Infectious Diseases Laboratory at Weymouth.

10 Progression Chapter

In the second and third season, it is probably best to move on to slightly harder waters, while keeping the easy one in reserve for the occasional trip when you need a bit of encouragement. Don't look for the really hard water—yet—, but try to find an average club or day ticket water where the carp are caught fairly regularly, but which contains a better average size of fish compared with your first water. There are plenty of good lakes about—especially in the south east of the country!—which contain a good head of carp between 8 and 15lbs, with some upper doubles and perhaps the odd twenty. Choose one where the carp are caught quite regularly, but which also offers a bit of a challenge, with a few problems to be solved, and some bigger fish to be landed.

You may have to fish more often, and perhaps to make up your mind to do longer sessions as well. This is not usually essential, but if you can stay for 12 hours, or even perhaps 24 hours, you ought to be able to cover at least one feeding period. You may also have to do more night fishing, especially if the water is heavily fished, which it is likely to be if it contains the sort of carp mentioned above. This will be useful to you, as you will get more practice in longer sessions after dark. You may also need practice in staying awake, while you will also find out if you can doze on a bed chair, yet still wake up quickly enough not to miss fish on the strike. If you can't do this, then don't attempt to sleep, but stay awake and concentrate for as long as you can; then, if it becomes too much, pack up and go home. Don't use a bivvy, but make yourself comfortable for a longer stay with a good umbrella and bed chair.

It will probably not be necessary to change the tackle very much, as I don't suggest you get onto a really long range water yet. On most waters you will be able to catch these carp at distances of up to 60 yards, and this is quite a long cast; test it in a field, and you may well find that you can't yet cast much further than this anyway. Don't convince yourself that this slightly harder water *must* be fished at such distances, though; some of the hardest waters produce good fish at short and medium range to those who think about their carp fishing, and do not just belt a bait into the far distance for the sake of it.

The same rig and set up will also be good enough for most waters, but remember that you may get into some quite heavy fish, so you will need to play them a bit circumspectly, and make sure that all your gear is in perfect condition; few things could be worse than losing what might be by far your best carp yet through a tackle failure.

Bread may well be 'fished out' in this type of water, but any of the other baits I have mentioned, especially luncheon meat and trout pellet paste, will probably work. If your bait has not been used much, a bit of pre-baiting will be needed; the quantity to introduce depends on the size of the water and the number of fish present, so it is impossible to advise on this, but if you are still not catching after putting in 200-300 baits in a known carp holding area, and fishing with them for a number of trips, you may have to change your bait.

Having tried all those mentioned, you might now have to start using simple high protein baits, mainly because others will be doing this. However, do try the standard baits first, as they still catch on many waters of this kind, and even on quite hard waters, for that matter. I won't give detailed advice on HP baits here, but you will find this information in the bait chapter or in the 'advanced' section by Kevin Maddocks. To get really high protein values your baits need to be based on either sodium caseinate, casein, or calcium caseinate, and sodium caseinate is also useful as a binder, even if you still use pet foods as the basis for your bait, as many of the top carp men do anyway. High protein values won't help much if the bait is not palatable, so it needs to have a good smell and flavour.

Kent carp angler Ron Middleton with a 22.10 caught at long range.

Problems which you may meet on this 'average' water are:
1. Takes are shorter and more wary, in which case you will
need to fish with closed bale arms—and the anti-reverse *off*,
remember—and strike quickly, although this is not by any
means always so on this kind of water;
2. If the carp have been caught a lot, they may tend to
'twitch' the bait a lot because they can feel the stiffness of
the monofilament nylon when they hold the bait in their lips,
which they may do cautiously if they have been caught
often. One way of beating this is to use a Terylene link of
about 12" or so attached to your end tackle, onto which the
hook is tied. It may look to you as if the fish will see this
much more easily than monofilament nylon, and in fact they
can see it, but they can see quite fine nylon also, so it doesn't
matter. What does affect the result is that the Terylene is
many times softer than the nylon, so they take the bait in
more easily and are less likely to feel it across their lips;

TERYLENE LINK

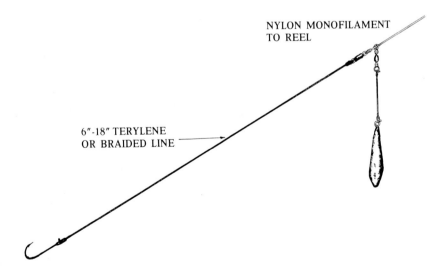

NYLON MONOFILAMENT
TO REEL

6"-18" TERYLENE
OR BRAIDED LINE

3. Playing the fish may take longer, and you will need a big enough net;

4. You may find problems because of overcrowding. You will have to learn to fish near others without casting across their tackle, or otherwise upsetting them. However, whenever possible look for the less busy areas of the lake; it may be that these are not fished because they are unproductive areas, but you won't know until you fish them, and you may well find good places which others have neglected for various reasons;

5. You will need to think very much more about your fishing. Spend all your blank periods trying to think up reasons why you may not be catching fish, and what you can do to affect the result. It may be necessary to change baits quite often, for example, and you may also find that there are definite feeding periods which you will need to fish if you want to succeed. These can often be in the very early mornings, or late at night, which means fishing at these times, whether you want to do so, or not;

6. You may not have been able to find a water of the right type which is a carp-only water, and the good mixed fishery will give you problems with other species taking the baits. If it is a mixed fishery producing good sized carp, it will probably contain good tench and bream also—chub are even worse! All these fish like carp baits, and will take quite big ones. You then need to look for hard baits, and one way to make these is by mixing them with eggs instead of water. The baits are then rolled into balls and dipped in boiling water for 1-3 minutes. When they dry and cool, a hard skin forms on the outside of the bait, and this helps to defeat other species. Carp anglers call these baits 'boilies'. Only certain mixes will boil really well—again you will find full details of recipes, and how to make these baits, in the bait chapter.

Boilies are boring and time consuming to prepare, so don't start using them until you have to. If you are getting many takes, and not hooking fish, change to a smaller hook and bait, and if you then catch lots of tench, bream and chub —or even large roach, then it may be time to go over to hard baits. The same applies if you are catching other species often on your normal carp baits.

Make sure that you don't choose, for this stage of your carp fishing at least, a water where there are too few carp compared with these other species. These are not carp waters, and pose many problems which should be left until you have had more experience. I knew of one water where three carp anglers caught 500 tench, and only 18 carp, in a season; leave this sort of water until later.

If you do have to use boilies, or any other hard type of bait, remember to ensure that the point, barb and bend of the hook are not obscured by the bait, as it is hard to strike through this type of bait.

METHOD OF HOOKING BOILIE FOR STANDARD LEGER RIG

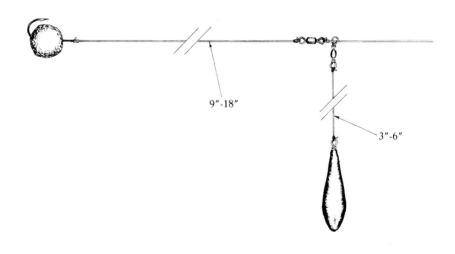

9"-18"

3"-6"

On such waters, and in warm weather, the fish may still take floating baits, but they will probably have learnt not to take floating crust. In this case, there are two other kinds of floating baits you can use. Your normal paste baits can usually be made to float by mixing them with eggs, adding baking powder and cooking them in the oven. Full details in the bait chapter. The second type of floater is anything edible which floats. Marshmallows, puffed wheat, some types of packeted crisps, but above all, the hard cat foods such as Go-Cat and Munchies. Thrown into the water, these floating pet foods, which have a very strong smell, seem to be almost immediately attractive to carp—and to other species. On one water where I used them, carp, tench, rudd, roach, moorhens, coots, ducks, dabchicks, seagulls and water rats all took them, eventually to the extent that they simply couldn't be used as carp baits!

The simplest way of fishing them seems to be soaking them in water for a short while, then putting them on the hook, with a float or controller to aid casting. I have seen

Peter with a good twenty which he caught in August 1982 whilst writing this book.
This leather took a multiple bait at medium range. Photograph by Roger Emmet.

non-carp anglers on many waters catching good carp like this. On other waters, carp seem to see the line or the different shape of the bait with the hook in it, and will take only the free offerings. It is possible to beat this trend by using a small piece of polystyrene—I've even had some success with cork—on the hook, which helps the bait to float, or by using two or three pieces at a time. Finally, if they won't take any other way, you can superglue the pet food piece to the back of the hook, although again you may have to use a piece of polystyrene to make the bait float. Be careful of that superglue, though; if you are not, you may end up in hospital having your fingers 'unstuck' by a surgeon!

Needless to say, these floating baits can all be used on a leger, like legered crust. As they are buoyant, they will float above the weight, and are very attractive to fish swimming in mid water or near the bottom.

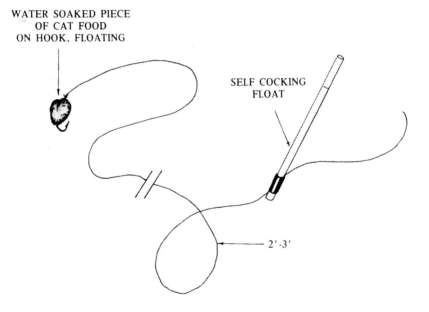

WATER SOAKED PIECE
OF CAT FOOD
ON HOOK, FLOATING

SELF COCKING
FLOAT

2'-3'

FLOATING MULTIPLE BAIT RIG

Do remember that you may not need to get onto HP baits or boilies. I know of many waters I would class as 'average', compared with the 'easy' one you fished last season, and the 'hard' ones you will fish in the future, where the standard baits, especially luncheon meat, TP paste, and pastes made from pet foods mixed with stiffeners, work very well, so give them a good try first—even if others are already using more complicated baits. Many anglers use these HP baits and boilies without needing to do so, simply because it is the fashion, and they hear of so many really big carp being caught on them. I am trying to get readers of this book to ignore the carp fishing fashions, and to use the tackle, methods and baits which catch fish.

A final point before we get on to the more advanced methods. So many anglers are tempted to take short cuts, and you may be tempted also. 'I'll read the advanced chapter first', you may think to yourself, 'then I can go straight on to the big fish catching, leaving out the rest.'

This is a very great mistake. Start in the hard water, and you may catch so few carp, like many people who write to me to ask for help, that you will give up carp fishing very quickly. Even if you have the help of friends who are experienced carp anglers, and can, with their help, miss out the early stages, and use advanced rigs and baits from the beginning, and catch 50 doubles in your first season, you may well lose much of the true pleasure of carp fishing. Most anglers I know who have started in this way, with great success with big fish straight away, have 'burnt themselves out' after a few seasons. They've done it all—they have nothing to look forward to; there is no challenge left. What is important is to try to succeed in catching the best fish your chosen water contains, whether they are 9 pounders or 29 pounders. Most of the waters I fish with my friend Roger Emmet are not big fish waters—there are almost none of these in our part of the country—but we put as much thought and effort into doing as well as we can on these waters, regardless of the size of the fish. If you do the same, this approach will be most useful to you if you do ever get onto the really big fish water.

Perhaps worse still, they may eventually, after 30 blanks at a hard water, get into a very big fish, and lose it through lack of experience in hooking, playing and landing smaller ones. I am convinced that my own enjoyment in carp fishing comes because I spent my first few years catching many small carp, as I have advised you to do, in easy waters, before I moved on to harder waters and bigger fish. This has made me a carp angler for life, and not just until I have caught so many doubles and 20's that I give it up because they no longer interest me. I had a friend once who wanted a 20, then a 30, followed by a 40, and then, he said, he would give up carp fishing. Because of my earlier experiences with small carp on light tackle, my attitude is the opposite: after catching my biggest carp in 1969, a thirty pounder from Ashlea Pool, one of the hardest carp waters in the country—in fact in the 'super-difficult' category, I was out the next week at my Devon lakes, catching 6lb commons on floating crust, and really enjoying it! Many people simply couldn't see how I could do this; they don't know what they are missing.

So, if you will take my advice to proceed by stages, you will almost certainly become a true carp angler, not just someone who fishes for 'results', and gives it all up once you've caught the biggest you can.

I don't suppose I shall convince many people that my way is the right way, judging by the letters I get from so many anglers who have never even caught small carp, yet who say to me they are determined to catch a 20 next season, but at least I have done my best to do so.

11 The Bait Chapter

I wasn't going to write a special chapter about bait in this book, partly because I have mentioned baits in other parts of the book, but also because I want to try to persuade the reader not to place too much emphasis on bait. Most beginners I come across, and many of the more experienced, seem to think that all they need is a 'secret' HP bait, and they will catch as much as any of the top carp anglers in the country. This is not so; angling ability is the key to success, along with experience, although on some hard waters, where you are competing with others who have good baits, it may help a lot if yours are at least as good.

First of all we have the standard baits already listed: bread, luncheon meat, sausage meat, pet food pastes, trout pellet paste, and sweet corn. Then the other multiples, and finally medium protein and high protein baits. Cheese, worms and potatoes will also catch carp.

As a basis for HP baits I suggest using sodium caseinate, which is much cheaper bought in bulk. Get together with some friends, and buy a 25 kilo bag. You should also buy a quantity of wheat germ, and Phillips Yeast Mixture, a budgie tonic, is another good buy, and some wheat gluten. A typical bait of this kind would be 3oz sodium caseinate, 3oz wheat germ, 2oz PYM and 1oz of milk powder.

In mixed fisheries and those with many small carp you will need a boiled bait. A typical recipe would be: 3oz sodium caseinate, 3oz wheat germ, 1oz Nukamel, 1oz brewers yeast, 2oz fish meal.

Instead of using water, use eggs for the whole amount of liquid needed. The amount to use will depend on the dry mix, so you will need to experiment with this. To give some idea, the bait I'm using at present takes about 80% of liquid, that is, 8oz of liquid for a 10oz dry mix.

Mix the dry ingredients well in a bowl, then break the eggs into a measuring jug. Beat the eggs well, then add a flavour if you are using one. Sweeteners are also very popular at present: brown sugar will do, at a rate of two dessert spoons to a 10oz mix. Don't forget that the total amount of liquid (eggs, flavour and sweetener, which can be liquidised by adding a very small amount of boiling water to the sugar, and stirring well) should not add up to more than the 80%, or whatever the amount needed with the dry mix.

Put the liquid onto the dry ingredients, then knead with the hands until a good sticky paste is formed. Be warned, it will be sticky, and it will take a bit to get it off your hands. Then knead into a large ball, being careful to press out all the air, or the bait may float.

Then pull off a small piece, and roll it into a ball between the palms of the hands, of the size required. If it is still too 'tacky' and the bait sticks to your hands so much that it won't roll well, it will be necessary to add some dry mix, but keep a note of the weight, so that you will know how much to use next time. If it is too dry, you will find that there are cracks in the bait ball once it is rolled, in which case it will not boil well, and a little more liquid must be added. A little water will be all right here.

Once the bait is just right, roll the balls of the size required (I have used boiled baits of from ¼ inch in diameter to one inch). Then boil a saucepan of water and lower the bait balls into it. I use a vegetable strainer and do about 50 baits at a time. Keep the water boiling while the baits are in it, and boil for 1 to 3 minutes—mine are usually done for 1½ minutes. Now lift the baits out, and tip them onto a smooth cloth. Roll them over after a few seconds, or you may get a soft spot where the water collects against the cloth. Now allow to cool. When all the baits are done and have cooled, leave them out to harden for about 12 hours if you want them at their hardest.

Since this is a long and messy business, try to do plenty at a time. I do 200-500, and keep them in the freezer, where they will keep fresh until needed.

Remember to hook them as shown, or you may miss on the strike.

It is not worth going to all this trouble if soft pastes or other baits are working well, but once other fish are being a nuisance, it may be best to use boiled baits all the time. They will last much longer, both on the hook and as free offerings, they won't fall off on the cast, and they do catch carp, although other species will get onto them eventually.

Flavours. If the bait has a good natural smell and taste, a flavour may not be needed, at least at first. PYM has a good natural smell, and so does fish meal such as herring meal, which is also worth buying in quantity as a basis for baits. If the bait is very bland, use a flavour, and this can also be added to a mix once the original bait seems to be catching fewer fish.

Food flavours are very good, and some of those which I have found to work well are: caramel, bun spice, maple, cinnamon and strawberry. 10ml (two teaspoonsful) is the most normally used for a 10oz mix; 5ml is usually about right, and some flavours are so strong that only half this may be needed. When in doubt, use less, rather than more. Too much flavour can cause the fish to 'spit' the bait. In these quantities, this type of flavour, which is used in the foods we eat, cannot possibly do any harm to the fish or to the water.

There are also many additives which can be mixed with the bait. Some of the commonest are: Marmite, curry powder, pilchard oil, Oxo, soy bean oil and sardines (savoury); others are: brown sugar, coffee, Dextrose, treacle, honey, condensed milk and glycerin (sweet).

There are many other flavours and additives, of course, and as complete a list as you are likely to find is in the bait chapter in 'Carp Fever', by Kevin Maddocks and John Baker.

Floaters. I don't use these at present, but will quote a recipe and method from 'Carp Fever':

4oz pilchard flavour Munchies
3oz sodium caseinate

½ teaspoon of baking powder
8 eggs

Mix the Munchies with the sodium caseinate and the baking powder. Beat the eggs in a separate mixing bowl. Mix together, and when the consistency of thick soup is formed, pour the contents into a well greased baking tin and bake in a medium/hot oven for 20 to 30 minutes.

This should float well, and is a very attractive bait to carp which will not take floating crust.

Multiple floaters. These are the floating pet foods already mentioned. They are not easy to fish and on some of our waters we have used the small floaters to get the carp going on the surface, then have fished small pieces of floating crust amongst them. This has been most successful once the carp adjust from the small amount of 'suck' required to take in the pet food floaters, to the larger amount needed for the floating crust, and the crust is much easier to fish.

Bait colours. I don't normally worry about this at all, as it does not seem to make much difference on my waters. Most of our baits are fairly light in colour, but on some waters dark baits seem to work best. Baits can be dyed by using black or brown food dyes. A red food dye also seems to work well; according to scientists, carp can see red, yellow and orange colours better than they can see green and blue. Green baits are picked up less easily by water birds, which can be a nuisance in shallow water, or when using floaters; not much use having them green if the carp can't see them, though!

12 More Advanced Carp Fishing

by Kevin Maddocks

Whilst there is no place in a book of this kind for too much detailed discussion of advanced carp fishing methods, if you have followed Peter's ideas in this book for the first two seasons, you may well want to fish harder waters for bigger carp and I hope to be able to help with this in this chapter. If you want more detailed information on my carp fishing ideas and methods, you will need to read my book 'Carp Fever',

Kevin with a 25½ pounder caught using the methods described in this chapter.
This fish took a single peanut fished on a hair rig.

where I have gone into much greater detail than is possible here.

It seems to me that there are basically three types of water which you might want to try now. They are:

1. Heavily fished waters containing large numbers of double figure carp, with some lower 20's. These are often club or season ticket waters, and may well be large gravel pits, especially in the south east;

2. The true big carp water, which contains fewer carp but where most of the fish are upper doubles and twenties; probably a mixed fishery;

3. Waters which contain very few, but very large carp, which live in a very rich water, and which are often pre-occupied for long periods with the abundant natural foods.

I should think that waters in the first category are most common.

Approach and Planning

For all the waters mentioned, it will probably be necessary to spend much more time at the water than you have done so far. More travelling may also be necessary, and it may take some time to discover the right type of water, except perhaps in the south east, where there are many waters of this kind. Feeding periods may not be very regular, and it is often necessary to spend periods of at least 24 hours, and possibly more, in order to be there when the fish are taking. I try to fit my fishing in with my normal life style, and as I am self employed I am able to go for a 48 to 72 hour session mid-week. Fifty hours, covering 3 days and 2 nights, is my favourite. Others have to settle for weekends, especially if they have to travel a long way to their chosen water.

I never use a bivvy of any kind, as I like to be very close to my rods. I am always determined to convert every possible take to a fish landed, and this can only be done if the angler is at his rods all the time. I use a bed chair, the legs of which have been specially adapted so that I can lie down, yet can reach my rods without moving from the bed chair. I am lucky in that I am able to sleep, yet can wake easily in time

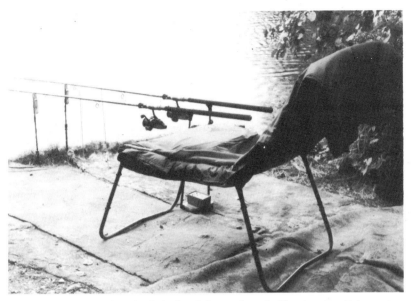

The KM set-up. Note the chair placed close to the rods. The carpets, which are commonplace on some Kent waters, are optional extras!

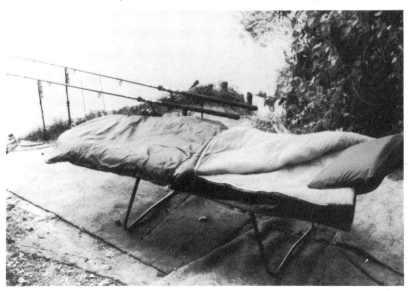

No bivvy, but ready for the night. Kevin can strike either rod without getting off the bed chair. The sleeping bag cover is waterproof and a brollie can be used in a tilted position to protect the top half of the body whilst not interfering with the strike.

to hook the fish, which I do without moving from the chair. I then sit up, slip my feet into my boots, and stand up to play the fish. I would recommend this system to all those who are now going to fish harder waters; if half the time is spent sound asleep in a bivvy, there is little point in spending so much time at the waterside, as many fish will be missed and lost. A further disadvantage of a bivvy is that you cannot keep a constant watch on the water for signs of feeding fish, etc.

It is necessary to be self sufficient, so take plenty of food and drink, and cooking materials if, like me, you like a hot meal on the bank, and regular cups of 'liquid gold', as my friend Ron Middleton calls it. It is often necessary to give up other interests if you are going to fish in this way, and to succeed on the harder waters. However, there are some waters where this sort of long stay fishing is not needed. Find out about this before you start, if possible.

Tackle

While the rods which Peter has suggested earlier will be useful to you for many years, you may now wish to buy another pair, and I recommend that these should be carbon fibre rods of 11ft in length, fairly fast in taper, which can be used at long range (70 yards plus). On some of these busy, large waters it will be necessary to cast 80 to 100 yards, and carbon fast tapers will enable you both to cast and to set the hook at these greater distances. I have had tremendous success with the KM range of rods made for me by Jack Simpson, of Simpsons of Turnford, and it is a fact that 90% of all carbon carp rods in use today are Simpsons KM's, or inferior copies based on them. I have used no other rods for years. Many hundreds have been sold to specialist carp anglers, and I give details of the range below.

Carbon Fibre Models

Fast Taper Models, one third tip action
11ft K.M.1 CF 2 piece. 2¼lb test curve
11ft K.M.2 CF 2 piece. 3lb test curve

Compound Taper, all-through action
11ft K.M.3 CF 2 piece. 1½lb test curve
11ft K.M.4 CF 2 piece. 2lb test curve

K.M. Dual Taper models
12ft K.M.2 D.T. 1¾lb test curve
11ft K.M.5 D.T. 1¾lb test curve

All models are two piece, black in colour and are available as rods, rod kits (handle finished) and blanks. Simpson's of Turnford are the sole manufacturers and retailers of KM rods, kits and blanks.

Either of the two most powerful 11ft models, or the 12 footer, will be ideal for long range fishing, and for coping with the large fish on this type of water. Where leads of over one and a half ounces are required to achieve the distance, a shock leader is necessary in most cases to prevent 'cracking off' during the cast. For maximum distance, a fairly light line of around seven or eight pounds BS, but no less than six pounds (governed by the action of a long range rod) should be used when the situation permits. To this, a heavier line, which will withstand the continued casting of a heavy lead, is attached by means of a four turn water knot. The minimum length of the shock leader should be so that when the angler is in his casting position there remains at least four turns of

FOUR TURN WATER KNOT
(FOR ATTACHING SHOCK AND SNAG LEADERS)

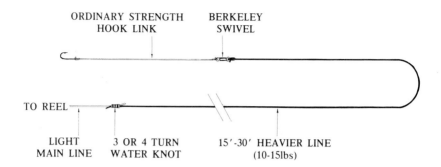

ORDINARY STRENGTH   BERKELEY
HOOK LINK   SWIVEL

TO REEL

LIGHT   3 OR 4 TURN   15'-30' HEAVIER LINE
MAIN LINE   WATER KNOT   (10-15lbs)

SHOCK LEADER FOR LONG RANGE CASTING
CAN ALSO BE USED AS A 'SNAG LEADER' TO PREVENT LINE FROM BEING
FRAYED OR CUT WHEN FISHING OVER SHARP GRAVEL BARS

the heavier line on the spool of the reel. This is the minimum acceptable length—I prefer a shock leader longer than this, usually about three rod lengths in length, so that when the fish is being played in the margins the shock leader knot is already on the spool instead of passing backwards and forwards through the rod rings. The type of leger stop for long range casting needs to be substantial and I continue to use a small Berkeley swivel in the line as I normally do. This also allows the angler to vary easily his type of line for the hook length. My usual choice for very long range casting is eight pounds BS Sylcast for the hook length and main line, and 15 pound BS Sylcast for the shock leader, in conjunction with a two ounce bomb. Continual casting with heavy leads causes wear and damage to the knot on the stop swivel. This is easily overcome by using a small plastic bead that will pass over the knot and rest on the eye of the swivel.

I would never fish seriously for carp without using an alarm no matter how short the session. I have lost count of the carp I have caught as a result of observation whilst I am fishing. Scores of carp have fallen to my rods either by casting to jumping fish, or by moving swim. I would definitely not have caught these fish had I not been using buzzers.

All my rods have line clips as shown in the diagrams.

LINE CLIP TO RETAIN LINE WHEN USING OPEN BALE ARM

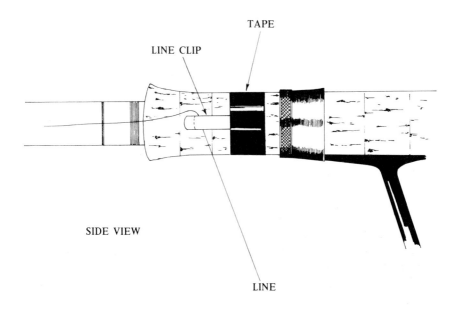

The first is used to stop line spillage from the spool when an open bale arm is used. These line clips are plastic and are made from shirt collar stiffeners—the type which are about two inches in length and a little less than a quarter of an inch wide. The stiffener is cut in two, a little off centre, so that one part is an eighth to a quarter of an inch longer than the other. These are then taped to the side of the rod handle just in front of the reel, with the longer part outermost. This enables you to separate the two plastic strips more easily in the dark. It is best to have about three quarters of an inch of clip protruding out in front of the tape as shown. For long range carp fishing my rods are fitted with drag clips which are taped onto the rods in such a position that they are a little in front of the buzzer head once the rod is in the rests. These are used for two purposes. The first is that when fishing at very long range there is a tendency for the

The most popular bite indication set-up used by experienced carp anglers today.
When there is a take, the indicators will move up and down the needle
while the 'buzzers' sound.

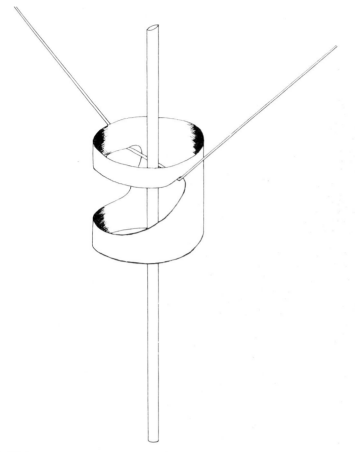

THE TYPE OF BITE INDICATOR USED BY KEVIN, SHOWING THE PATH OF THE
LINE. THIS INDICATOR WILL EITHER STAY ON THE LINE, OR WILL DROP OFF,
DEPENDING ON THE LENGTH OF THE 'NEEDLE'. THESE SOFT, WHITE INDICA-
TORS ARE MADE FROM PLASTIC WINE BOTTLE TOPS. IF YOU DO NOT WISH
TO MAKE YOUR OWN THEN SIMILAR ONES ARE AVAILABLE, COMPLETE WITH
NEEDLE, FROM MOST SPECIALIST ANGLING SHOPS AND ARE MANUFACTURED
BY GARDNER TACKLE.

indicator to creep continually upwards, caused by excessive
underwater drag, and this is easily overcome by using this
clip. Its other use, which I would only recommend you to put
into practice at a later stage in your carp fishing career, is
when using the advanced rigs and here the drag clip can be
used to further the effectiveness of them especially when

DRAG CLIP TAPED TO ROD IN FRONT OF BUZZER TO COUNTERACT DRAG,
OR FOR USE WITH ADVANCED RIGS

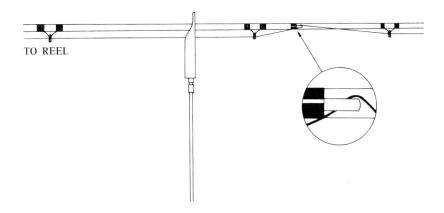

TO REEL

the fish 'wise up' to these bolt and 'hair' rigs. But until you fully understand the way carp feed, why these rigs work and when it is the right time to use them you would do better to leave this until much more experience is gained. If you do not wish to make your own line clips, similar ones have recently become available from most specialist angling shops and are manufactured by John Roberts and Gardner Tackle. The remainder of the tackle need be little different from that already recommended, and details of rigs etc. will be given later. I use standard Sylcast line and, for most of my fishing, Au Lion d'Or hooks.

Baits

I have caught carp to over 30lbs on the standard baits mentioned by Peter, especially on luncheon meat or baits made from pet foods such as Munchies; in fact, many of my baits are still Munchie based. However, it is best now to be able to make up high protein or high nutritive value baits based on sodium caseinate or Casilan and I give two sample recipes below.

4oz Casilan   5oz Sodium Caseinate
2oz Complan   1oz Lactalbumin

1oz Lactalbumin	1oz Wheat Gluten
2oz C & G Baby Milk	1oz Equivite
1oz Wheatgerm	2oz Soya Flour

I would never advise HP or HNV baits without saying that a bait doesn't need to be high in nutritional value, expensive, or difficult to obtain to be a very successful one. If you want to prove this to yourself or you simply wish to use a different base mix when everyone else is on HNV baits, try the following simple recipe adding eggs and flavour in the normal way:

8oz Semolina
4oz Soya Flour

Once a good base is discovered, it can often be used for several years, with only the flavour being changed when needed. Here is a list of some of the most successful flavours I have come across, and where they can be obtained.

Cream: Geoff Kemp, Pilgrims Court, Days Lane, Pilgrims Hatch, Brentwood, Essex.

Maple: Kohnstamms, 76 Glentham Road, London SW13.

Milk: Dubuis & Rowsell, Duroma Works, Elmwood Road, Croydon, Surrey.

Bun Spice 'B': Underwood & Barker, Billericay, Essex.

Cinnamon: Rayners, Commercial Road, Edmonton N18 1TQ.

Strawberry: Rayners, Commercial Road, Edmonton N18 1TQ.

Do not make the flavours too strong, as Peter has already said—10ml (2 teaspoons) is usually the maximum; more may prevent the fish from taking the bait. A more common amount is 5ml, 1 teaspoonful, to a 10 ounce mix of bait, but this does really depend on the individual flavour—one of my favourites I use at a concentration of 15ml to a 10oz mix. With this same flavour (cream) I have had tremendous success by adding even 20ml to a mix but this will only work well if a liquid sugar is added, such as 10ml Hermasetas, to counteract the bitterness of the bait and make it more acceptable to the carp. I must stress, however, that this is an exception and when most flavours are added at a concentration of more than 10ml, results become poorer. If, like me, you taste all your finished baits you can play around with the concentrations of flavour and sugars and providing it doesn't taste very strong, i.e. hot, bitter or sour, it will almost certainly be acceptable to the carp. Finally, a point worth noting—the amount of flavour I have mentioned is for boiled baits and I would not advise more than 5ml in a soft paste mix.

All my baits now are boiled; I don't use soft pastes. They are mixed with eggs only, in the quantities advised. Once they are rolled into balls, the baits are dipped into a saucepan of boiling water for 1-2 minutes and allowed to cool and dry. Make sure all of the air is squeezed out of the bait when preparing it, or the baits may float after boiling if it happens to be a very light mix, as already described in the Bait Chapter.

I find small baits of about ¼-½inch in diameter work best, but they can be made larger. If fishing at long range they will need to be no less than ½ inch diameter as smaller baits are very difficult to catapult any real distance. I leave mine laid out on a worktop or table for at least 12 hours, as Peter recommends, when they become much harder. Don't worry if a bait is hard; the harder the better. I find that it is the hardness of the boilie that puts the smaller fish off and not its size as many carp anglers believe.

Two good floater recipes are:

3oz Soya Flour	1oz Yestamin
2oz Self Raising Flour	2oz Sodium Caseinate
2oz Casein	2oz Soya Flour
1oz Wheat Gluten	2oz Wheat Germ
1oz Sodium Caseinate	½ teasp. Baking Powder
1oz Corn Meal	

add flavour as required

I have had some very good fish on floating multiple baits such as the pet food mentioned earlier and unless the fish are taking very confidently I superglue one to the back of the hook and put a small piece of polystyrene in the hole (see diagram) to counteract the weight of the hook. To aid casting I fish them with a controller, which is a weighted float fixed

FLOATING CAT FOOD WITH CONTROLLER

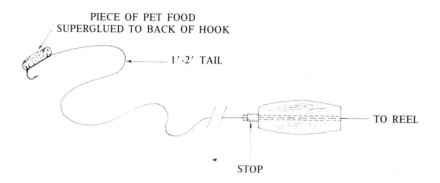

PIECE OF PET FOOD
SUPERGLUED TO BACK OF HOOK

1'-2' TAIL

TO REEL

STOP

about 12″ from the bait. Controllers can be carved from wood such as mahogany or a loaded, self cocking float does the job nicely.

I will now deal with the three categories of water listed in turn, starting with:

1. Heavily fished club and season ticket waters, often large or fairly large gravel pits, containing a good number of doubles, with some 20's.

The main problem with this type of water arises from the fact that as it is so heavily fished, the fish are caught several times each season, and they have become quite hard to catch.

It will be necessary to 'compete' with other very experienced carp anglers, who know the water well. If possible, try to do something different from the others. Fish areas where they don't go, or cannot cast to; use different baits, perhaps even a simpler one than they are using. If they use small baits, try large ones, and vice versa. Fish as many rods as are allowed on the water—usually only two nowadays. Many carp anglers find pre-baiting beneficial so if success does not come quickly you can try this. Using my own baits I very rarely find pre-baiting necessary, although on some waters I may throw in as many as 100 baits when I start my 2 or 3 day session. If it is the type of water that receives scores of different baits during each season then it will not be necessary to educate the fish into taking a new one—in fact on most of these waters a new bait is accepted immediately and is often the most successful. On these types of waters I rely completely on my fishing skill and often put no free offerings in at all especially when I think too much bait is being thrown in by others. I find by fishing in this way and making a concerted effort to put my bait right on top of the fish, success is almost a certainty.

It has been proved conclusively that it is often not the bait which prevents fish from taking on hard waters, but the feel of the stiff line over the lips of a taking carp. For this reason, on the harder waters, these regularly caught fish tend to carefully take the baits into their lips, and hold them, then expel them and do the same again. This produces 'twitches' on the indicator or sometimes no indication at all.

When fishing with boilies, this can often be beaten by using a bolt rig technique, although my own normal leger rig is the same as Peter's which you have seen earlier.

BOLT RIG

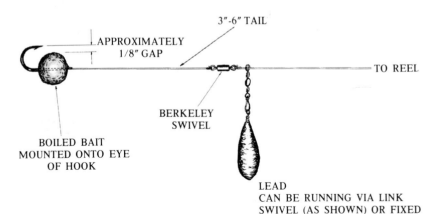

3″-6″ TAIL

APPROXIMATELY
1/8″ GAP

BERKELEY
SWIVEL

TO REEL

BOILED BAIT
MOUNTED ONTO EYE
OF HOOK

LEAD
CAN BE RUNNING VIA LINK
SWIVEL (AS SHOWN) OR FIXED

The object of the bolt rig is to 'panic' the carp into bolting with the bait once it feels the resistance of the lead, or the prick of the hook. Because of this, it is essential that the boilie be mounted as shown, with the bait pulled up onto the eye of the hook, while the bend and most of the shank is exposed. It is also important to have the hook big enough so that there is always a gap of about $\frac{1}{8}''$ between the bait and the point of the hook. If the point is obscured, you will not hook the fish. If you are using this rig, any sort of bites other than runs means the rig is not working properly and therefore they must be accepted. One normally has to make various adjustments until every indication is a run and these are one, or all, of the following: length of tail, 'proudness' of hook, use of line tight in drag clip or not, and the lead fixed or running.

If this fails, the 'hair rig' can be tried. This was developed after many experiments by Len Middleton and myself on carp in my tank at home to encourage carp to take a bait well back to the pharyngeal teeth while being unable to feel any line over their lips. The rig is set up as shown.

The line is tied to the bend of the hook, and $\frac{1}{2}$ to $1\frac{1}{2}$lb BS nylon is used. The bait can be tied on, or if it is a boilie, can be put on by inserting the 'hair' via a needle, and then tying a slip-knot and pulling it tight around the bait. Alternatively, a small loop can be tied at the end of the 'hair' and after being pulled through the bait with a needle, a $\frac{1}{4}''$ length of heavy line or cocktail stick can be put through the loop and the bait pulled down firmly against it, so that the heavy piece of line or cocktail stick sinks into the bait a little. The distance from the bend of the hook to the centre of the bait should be no more than 2 inches, and 1 to $1\frac{1}{2}$ inches is usually best. Takes are very confident by this method, so either fish with an open bale arm or with the bale arm closed and the anti-reverse off, when the reel can 'churn' if you cannot strike in time. I personally never fish 'churner' style but many carp anglers do. Bite-offs are almost impossible, as the hook only gets inside the mouth, and almost every fish is hooked just inside the mouth. Use small hooks in this

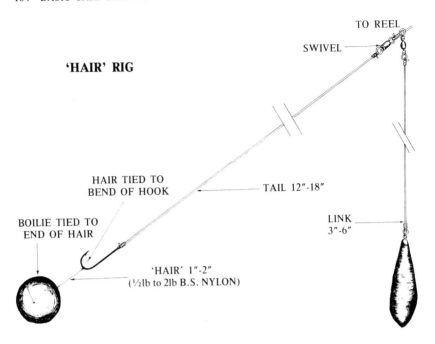

'HAIR' RIG

TO REEL

SWIVEL

HAIR TIED TO
BEND OF HOOK

TAIL 12″-18″

BOILIE TIED TO
END OF HAIR

LINK
3″-6″

'HAIR' 1″-2″
(½lb to 2lb B.S. NYLON)

case—either 6's or 8's. I've had plenty of carp up to over 30lbs using these small hooks—once they take hold, they don't come out.

This rig, and indeed the bolt rig, is *only* needed in hard waters where carp twitch at baits. Do *not* use them on easy waters where baits are taken in the normal manner.

If you are still not catching on these hard fished waters, you may need to take up golf!

2. This is the big fish water, which may not be quite so hard fished, as fewer fish are caught, but will be fished very well and often by the experienced carp anglers who want to catch these big fish, many of which will be 20's. This sort of water is less common, and probably harder to get into, as many have limited memberships. Fewer fish can be expected, and I do not really advise fishing this type of water until you have had a season or two catching plenty of good doubles with perhaps the odd lower 20 on waters in category one. However, if you have a water of this type which you can get

Ron Middleton demonstrates a long range cast. This is the starting position . . .

. . . and the cast finishes like this. In this case the bait went 'only' about 95 yards,
but Ron can do more, and with remarkable accuracy also.

into, and you feel that you can face the long blank periods which are bound to occur, then a water of this kind may be worth trying.

Tackle, baits and methods are likely to be as recommended for category one, but there may be some opportunities for opportunist stalking, especially in hot weather.

3. This is the very rich, sometimes small water, which contains few, but very large carp, with perhaps a thirty or two. Again I suggest some experience in the other two categories before you try this type. If you do fish a water in this category, the main problem is likely to be that the fish are often preoccupied with natural foods, and will have to be offered something very attractive as a bait if they are going to take it. On the smaller waters of this kind, the fish may often be very close to the banks, and much of the fishing will not be static—if you settle down in one place, those big fish may not come to the area for several weeks, which is a long wait by any standards! Observation is very important in waters of this kind; often you will be casting to visible fish, and it will be essential to learn the habits of the fish and their holding and feeding areas, if you are to have any chance of catching them. I have found that spending considerable

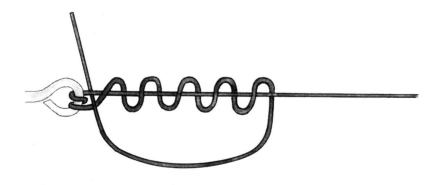

K.M. TYPE BLOOD KNOT

time sitting up trees can be most rewarding. Any of the rigs and methods may succeed, and so may even the most basic methods mentioned, such as a freelined bait fished at short range on a single rod. There are often literally weeks without a carp being caught, and it is often best to alternate fishing this very hard type of water with a category one water where some reasonable fish are not quite so hard to get onto the bank.

Concentration, being near to the rods, and much thought are necessary for success with more advanced fishing. I keep detailed records of everything which happens when I fish, even quite small takes. I then spend much time analysing the information in order to improve my results next time I fish. Plan all trips carefully, and leave nothing to chance. Spend all the time when there is no action working out what you can do to improve the results. Watch the water carefully, and be prepared to move all your gear, even several times, if there is reason to believe that you are not going to catch where you are, or that you might catch elsewhere. Remember there is always room for improvement and if you want to be a successful carp angler you must be striving to find these improvements all the time no matter how well you are doing.

Peter has already recommended the reader to join the CAA, and I endorse this; it will be very valuable to you. I also strongly advise any carp angler who has done two or three seasons successful carp fishing to apply to join the British Carp Study Group, of which the author of this book is Secretary, and I am Assistant Secretary. Peter founded this national organisation for carp anglers in 1969, and the start of the BCSG was, in fact, the beginning of organised carp fishing in this country. Since then, the BCSG and CAA have published more than 50 magazines between then, and this was also the beginning of carp fishing literature.

The BCSG is an independent, non-political organisation, which is one of the things I like about it; at BCSG meetings and Conferences the talk is of carp and carp fishing. There are no rules and regulations, and no formal meetings. Most of the leading carp anglers in this country, and in several other countries, are members, or have been members, of the BCSG, and at present there are 250 members. Meetings are held in most parts of the country, and there are also national social meetings, Conferences, a BCSG Book, and three free magazines a year—for members only.

The idea of the BCSG is not an elitist organisation, but because it is selective, and is hard to get into, it gives the experienced carp angler something to aim at; if he is accepted as a BCSG member, he has really achieved something. There are no membership qualifications, and the angler's results are considered in the context of where he lives and fishes.

The BCSG means a lot to me and I will repeat what I wrote in Carp Fever 3 years ago, "...for joining the BCSG has been one of the best things I have done in my carp fishing career."

Finally, I want to support Peter's pleas for readers of this book not to attempt to take short cuts, and be tempted to go straight to this chapter, and to start at the 'wrong' end of carp fishing. Even if you succeed—and it is more likely that you will lose big fish if you have no experience of catching smaller ones—you may well soon give up because of fishing too hard waters, while you will lose very much of the pleasure of carp fishing. Start at the beginning; follow the 'Mohan plan', and you will stand the best chance of becoming a successful carp angler—and, what is more, a carp angler for life.

13 Alphabetical Advice Chapter

Amino acids: All food, and indeed all living tissue, contains amino acids. It has been said that these added to baits will improve the ability to attract fish. Although some amino acid baits do work, I can find no evidence to suggest that these baits are worth using. Neither Kevin nor myself uses them, and they are not recommended, not least because if too much is used, amino acids can be POISONS. The exception is ready made-up, bought baits containing amino acids, which are safe to use and may be very good.

Bait: when in doubt, use simple baits. Persist for some time even if a bait is not catching.

Bait and flavour suppliers: see list of useful addresses for recommended bait or bait material suppliers. Remember that the more you can buy, the cheaper.

Barbless hooks: recommended on some waters; insisted in on a few; may damage fish less; try pinching barbs flat with pliers, but close your eyes when you do so, as the barb sometimes flies off.

BCSG Advisory Service: send to the BCSG for a questionnaire to help you with carp fishing problems; SAE essential.

Bite-offs: can occur when bait is taken past pharyngeal (throat) teeth; remedies—tight line, quick strikes, bolt rigs, 'hair' rig. The author has caught well over 3,000 carp and has never had a bite-off. If you get many, it is bad angling.

Buzzers: Do not use 'buzzers' if they annoy others; turn down sound so that only you can hear them; don't use normally without an indicator on the line.

Clubs: often have the best carp waters, but some don't like carp specialists. Usual reason given is that they behave too badly, but the true reason is that they are often too successful, showing up others who fish the waters! I am not getting at clubs generally here, of course—only at those which deliberately discriminate against carp anglers. There are some very good clubs in most parts of the country, and there are many who work very well with their carp fishing members, and who do a lot to help them with stocking, etc. Possibly the best of these is Lymm Angling Club, in Cheshire, which has some very good carp waters and a most enlightened attitude towards carp anglers. (Chairman: Peter Biles, 16 Hankinson Close, Partington, Urmston, Manchester M31.)

Cheating: don't cheat on fish weights or when reporting fish.

Countryside code: do shut gates, do nothing to annoy farmers, don't leave litter or line, and never make a noise or disturb people living nearby. Most carp lakes are in the country; if you cannot behave well in the countryside you should not go carp fishing. Pick up any discarded line you see, as this may save a bird's life.

Carp care: look after your hooked carp. Remove the hook carefully without damage, placing the carp on a soft bank or on a wet sack if the bank is a hard one. Never keep out of water for more than a few minutes. Hold the fish as little as possible. Do not keep in a sack or any other way if you can avoid it. Return carefully to the water, supporting the fish upright until it swims away. This applies to *all* carp, whatever their size.

Doubles: carp of over 10lbs are not the only carp which matter. I don't have a very high opinion of those who only 'count' doubles and twenties. A 9.15 is as good as a double any day, and might be better. Don't fish only for 'results', which means usually for doubles or twenties; fish for enjoyment—big fish are a bonus.

Float fishing: this has little place in modern carp fishing. After 10 years as a general angler I took up carp fishing partly to get away from having to fiddle about with floats. Can be used for close-in fishing in deepish waters when carp are swimming in mid-water, but carp will often not take as they can see the line too easily.

Estimating carp weights in water: this is very hard, even for the carp angler who has seen, and caught, plenty of big fish. Don't deceive yourself—almost every angler who contacts me tells me there are 20's and 30's in his water, even if none have been caught, he has never seen a fish of this size on the bank, and even if I know quite well the water contains nothing of this size! Only quote weights of fish which you can *prove* have been caught, not those you think you have seen, or others report having been caught, without any proof.

Ethics: when other people do something with which you disagree in carp fishing—especially if they catch better carp than you do through it!—it is *not* ethical; when *you* do something similar, it *is* ethical!

Foul-hooking: it is impossible to carp fish without occasionally hooking carp elsewhere than in the mouth. As long as you have not done this intentionally—and who would?—then don't let it worry you. Foul hooked carp fight very hard, and are good fish. Whether you 'count' them, depends on you; some do, some don't. Others count only carp hooked an inch or so from the mouth, while others never count a foul hooked fish—however big it is. As long as I have struck a take, and the hook is in the fish, I count them all!

Helping others: carp anglers seem to have a reputation as dour, silent, and even unpleasant people, although most carp anglers I know are not like this at all. Try to be friendly and helpful to others, especially to young people; one day, you may be glad of some help. If people, of any age, are really being a pest, of course, they don't deserve a friendly attitude. Don't rush to net others' fish—ask if help is required, and if the reply makes it clear you are not wanted, fade away! Carp anglers are often individualistic, and many prefer to be left alone. Never talk to carp anglers while they are setting up and casting out, and don't ask what bait they are using; they may not want to tell you. If *you* are asked, either tell, or say you would prefer not to, but don't lie to others.

High protein baits: although these have now been going into many waters in enormous quantities for nearly 15 years (about the whole of the growing period for the carp in those waters!) people can still be heard to say that they might damage carp! This is nonsense. Most are based on milk products, wheat germ (eaten in huge quantities by health food addicts!), eggs, animal food etc, and there is good evidence to show that they increase growth rates and feed the fish well.

Hooking fish on other people's rods: never strike anyone else's rod, unless you are asked to. If it is a close friend, and he is out of earshot, then it will probably be all right, unless you have an agreement not to do so. If it is a stranger, and he has a run, it is better to walk away and try to find him, even if he loses the fish; pick up that rod, and you may even be accused of trying to steal it! However, the decision is yours, and you may wish to take the risk if it means saving another angler's rod which is about to be pulled into the water.

Litter: we are a nation of filthy litter louts—go to any public place if you doubt me. Many club and day ticket waters are full of litter. Don't add to it. Take a bag and put ALL your litter in it, and take it home. I even take a plastic bag with me and pick up litter left by others, as I cannot stand seeing litter in the countryside. There are some good clubs, but on many no-one bothers about the litter, and the so-called 'bailiffs' are too lazy to enforce the rules, or to pick up the litter. Remember that line kills birds and other animals, so don't leave it.

Long stay fishing: whether we like to admit it or not, long stay carp fishing—more than a night or so—is really a form of camping at the water. If the angler is noisy and messy, and leaves his tins and other rubbish behind when he goes, this type of fishing can be offensive to others. Water owners often dislike it and it can spoil small waters, by having people present on the bank all the time. If you do get into this sort of fishing, try to be as unobtrusive as possible; when you leave, there should be no trace of your having been there.

Margin fishing: an 'old fashioned' method of carp fishing, with the rod in rests and a piece of crust attached to line dangling from the end and just in the water. Better to hold the rod if fishing in the margins.

Luck: 'Had any luck, mate?'. Most non-anglers and occasional anglers believe that success in angling is mainly due to 'luck'. The carp angler's definition of luck should perhaps be that it is luck when anyone else catches a good fish, but skill when he does the same! We all get both good and bad luck at times but I think luck plays little part in carp fishing. The most successful carp anglers achieve success wherever they fish; they catch good fish consistently from every water they choose to fish, so they don't need much luck. In fact, I suspect that this may be a 'lucky' book.

At the same time that I have been writing it, I have been having one of my best seasons ever for good fish—upper doubles and 20's are not very common in the south west, where I do nearly all my fishing. My friend and fishing companion, Roger Emmet, would also agree with the 'lucky book' tag; recently during a fishing trip, I asked him to read the book and make suggestions. Soon after starting, he had a lower double, and almost as soon as he picked up the manuscript after that, he had another. He had just stepped a foot or two away from his rods towards me, meanwhile saying 'It's no good . . .', expecting I would think he meant the book, when really he meant that it hadn't worked for the third time, as he'd done about half an hour without a take, when his buzzer sounded, he turned round, struck, and after a very hard fight landed an 18lb mirror—the third double while reading the manuscript, on a hard water! I hope it also proves a 'lucky' book for you, the reader.

Noise: although human speech is well within the range of a carp's hearing, ordinary voices may have no effect on carp especially when the angler is casting some way. However, all forms of noise do annoy other people, such as local residents and other carp anglers like myself who go fishing partly for peace and quiet, so don't make ANY noise. Don't shout across the lake to your friends, but go round and speak to them quietly. I think the quiet carp angler is likely to catch more carp, but even if you don't believe this, have some consideration for others.

Peas and beans, cooking: there is some evidence to suggest that if peas and beans (pulses) are uncooked or partly cooked, they may damage or even kill fish. Although I don't like bait bans, I have had to ban them on some of my waters. If you do use them, cook them as well as you would if they were for human consumption, and don't normally use them uncooked or partially cooked. Some do only need soaking, as it is the swelling caused by soaking which may harm fish.

Personal records: detailed records of your carp fishing *may* not help you to catch more carp, although they probably will, but even if they don't they are very useful to look back on—I have a record of every carp I have caught for over 30 years! Nearly all specialist carp anglers keep detailed records, and even those who catch enormous numbers keep a record of every fish they have caught, and the weight at least of every double. I strongly advise all readers to do the same. Apart from anything else, many anglers do not tell the truth about their catches—to put it politely!—and there are those who will suspect you also if you say you don't 'bother' to record numbers and weights.

Photographing: for the same reasons as those listed above, try to get a good picture of at least all your 'doubles'. Photos can also be used for identification purposes.

Polystyrene: this is that white stuff used for packing. Useful to have some in your tackle bag (see text).

Pre-baiting: rarely necessary in easy waters, but in harder waters it may have to be carried out when introducing a new bait, especially if other anglers are pre-baiting the water heavily. I am often asked how much to put in, but this depends entirely on the size of the water, the amount of fish it contains, and the size and number of other species. When in doubt—don't; just put 20-50 baits in when you start, and the same when you leave. It is often worth putting in this number of baits 24-48 hours before you fish the water, but only if this can be done without disturbing others—and if you can guarantee to get the baited swim!

Recommended waters: it is very difficult to recommend individual waters in a book of this kind. However, Leisure Sport have some very good carp waters; Waveney Valley Lakes, Wortwell, Norfolk are also very good (tel. Homersfield 530); William Boyer Fishing has some good waters in Bucks. and Middlesex, where CAA members receive a discount (send SAE to William Boyer Fishing, Trout Road, West Drayton, Middlesex, tel. West Drayton 44707); Llandrindod Wells Lake, Powys, Wales is heavily stocked with carp to over 20lb (contact Jim Chapman at the boathouse at the lake, tel. 0597-3404, which is in the town of Llandrindod Wells, for day and season tickets; excellent accommodation is available at a first class hotel near the lake from Peter Smith, the Metropole Hotel, Llandrindod Wells, tel. 0597-2881); Red Beck Lake Worcs. (season tickets only, contact the author at CAA/HQ); Oxenham Lakes, near Exeter, Devon (small syndicate, occasional vacancies, contact Peter Mohan for details); Brookfield Lane Lake, Cheshunt, Herts. (tickets from Simpsons of Turnford).

Publicity: this is up to the individual. Some like publicity, some don't. In fact, carp specialists very rarely report their catches these days, because publicity might draw attention to their waters. 95% of large carp caught are not reported to the angling press. The 250 members of the BCSG caught about 5,000 doubles, 500 twenties, 12 thirties and a forty pounder in the 1981-82 season; hardly *any* of these carp were reported! Make sure publicity is allowed on your water before you report anything, and if those who control the water don't want the location given away, then just report the catch without giving the water location. The weeklies are always pleased to hear from anglers who have make good catches. If you send pictures, good quality black and white prints are the best. Make sure you keep a copy as the angling papers are known to mislay them frequently after use. The monthly magazines may include some news, but are best for articles. Send them to the Editor, typed in double spacing on plain paper.

Record claims: record claims must be made to the British Rod Caught Record Fish Committee. An official of the Committee *must* see the fish, but you don't have to kill it; keep it alive, contact the BRFC, and get someone to come and see it. If you are not prepared to keep to the BRFC rules, don't claim, and don't expect them to change their rules for you! Some Water Authorities have local records, so contact your W/A if you wish to claim a local record; this also applies to club and water records. The *official* British record rod caught carp was a common which weighed 44lbs, and which was caught by Richard Walker in September, 1952.

Rod building: I am not qualified to give advice on building rods—I can hardly even put a light bulb in its socket without it falling out! Rod kits can be bought from most dealers, with the handles finished, and only rings have to be added. It is also possible to buy the blank in two sections, with the spigots already fitted, and the cork handle can also be bought, already shaped, and in sections. It is only necessary then to glue the handles on to the blank, and to rub them

PM's Terry Eustace Tackle Bag.

down. The rod rings must then be whipped on and the spigots also whipped to prevent splitting. Most dealers will be able to give advice on how to do this.

Re-catching carp: many carp are caught several times each season; far more often than some people think. I know of a double which was caught at least 8 times last season, and smaller fish are caught much more often. One of my waters is producing about 300 carp *a week*—and there are only about 300 in the water!

Rules: have to be careful what I say here, or I shall be accused of encouraging anglers to break rules. Of course you should keep to rules at all times, and if you break rules on syndicate waters you will very soon lose your membership, so never break a rule on a syndicate or private water. If you do—by mistake, or course!—break a rule on a club or day ticket water, at least do so in a way so that you won't get caught. If you are caught red-handed, don't be aggressive, but apologise and admit you were wrong. This way you may not get into too much trouble, but if you get aggressive, you will be out for sure!

Sacking carp: if possible, don't. If you must keep a fish to show to friends, or for photographing, put one fish only in a large industrial nylon sack which has plenty of holes in it, or a curtain mesh sack. Put in deep water in shade, and check frequently. Never keep a fish for more than a few hours. Please note that in some W/A areas it may actually be illegal to keep carp in sacks. Do not keep large carp in netting carp 'sacks' or keep nets.

'Sacks', Terylene curtain mesh: good cheap sacks can be made from Terylene curtain net mesh material. Make the sack large, stitch with a sewing machine, and insert a draw string with a long cord at the neck. I have used these for years, along with Kevin Nash industrial nylon carp sacks, and find both types very good.

Split shot: there is now some evidence to suggest that split shot may kill swans, although I am sure that shot from guns, and lead from boat motors, also kills. When possible, try not to use split shot at all.

Syndicate waters: many carp anglers seem to get the idea that once they can get into a syndicate, they will catch lots of big carp. In fact, most big carp are caught from club, season ticket and day ticket waters. Carp anglers join syndicates for different reasons. On a syndicate you will get a less heavily fished water, more peace and quiet, and stricter rules so that members get good, peaceful fishing. This is what you pay extra for, not necessarily big fish. You are only likely to get into a carp syndicate by knowing those who run the waters, and CAA and BCSG membership may help you here. CAA/BCSG members get preferential entry into all the waters I run, and possibly some others. There are two types of syndicates: one is where a group of people get together to rent a water, in which case all should have some say in what goes on. More common is the sort of water which is leased by one individual, who then organises a syndicate on the water. In this case he will run the water his way, as he pays the rent and takes the responsibility, and you will have to do as he says, or get thrown out!

Water Authority licences: A licence is essential for everyone in most waters, although in some areas young people under a certain age may not need them. You normally need a licence for each rod you use, and the use of more than two rods is not permitted on most waters these days. Licences can be bought from most tackle shops or direct from the Water Authority.

Waterside behaviour: this is dealt with elsewhere in the book. If the carp angler obeys the rules, is quiet, sensible and unobtrusive, does no damage, leaves no litter or line, does not harm wild life, and closes gates etc, he is likely to get on well with other anglers, officials, and riparian owners.

Water secrecy: carp anglers are often accused by others, especially by journalists, of being too secretive about where their catches are made. This is quite understandable for a journalist, as we must realise that it is part of their job to get the information, for publication in their paper or magazine for the benefit of their readers. However, carp anglers have now learnt by experience that there are times when they simply cannot risk giving the location of the waters where they have made good catches, which is why so many of the big carp catches are not reported.

I will quote just one case which illustrates the point: a well known carp angler finally caught a very big carp, after years of fishing one place in a hard water. He made the mistake of publicising this, with the result that he was unable to find a place to fish in the area where he had caught the big fish for the *next three months*. In that time, 11 more big carp were taken; he didn't get one of them!

Journalists must understand this point, while we should realise that we should, as far as possible, try to co-operate with the angling papers and give as much detail of catches as we can; it is partly for this information for which other anglers buy the angling papers and magazines.

Weighing carp: do this carefully in a *wet* weighing sling or sack. Weigh the sack first, and deduct this from the weight; don't cheat. I am a very good judge of carp weights, yet I am often told by an angler that his fish is several pounds heavier

First wet the weighing sling . . .

. . . and lay the fish on it . . .

. . . and it is ready for weighing. Put the hook of the scales through the rings, having first weighed the empty sling. This Kevin Nash weighing sling ensures that the fish cannot be damaged during weighing.

than I can see it is! Some members even claim fish from waters I control that I know quite well are heavier than anything which exists in the water, while I have seen a member claim a fish as a double, when I could see it wasn't, and in fact he didn't weigh it anyway! Many anglers tell me of doubles they have caught from my own waters, but when challenged, admit they didn't weigh the fish—usually because they knew quite well it wasn't a double, and didn't want to prove this to be so. In this way you are only cheating yourselves. I only believe the weights of carp when I have seen them weighed, or when the weight is reported by a reliable friend. Years of experience have taught me that many anglers lie about fish weights; don't be one of them. At first, weigh every fish carefully, and keep a record of the weights; don't lie or exaggerate.

Weed fishing: many inexperienced carp anglers are worried about fishing in weed. Provided heavy line is used (12-15lbs BS), it is quite possible to fish successfully for carp in the heaviest weed. The carp will smell the bait even if they can't see it. Remember that even those substances which don't smell strongly to us are easily detected by carp; I have often watched carp 'scent' floating crust even when it is resting on top of heavy weed, and seen them root about until they found it, pushing those lips up through the weed to engulf the invisible crust or HP floater. Takes may be short in weed, and you will have to hold the fish hard to prevent it from going far. Ashlea Pool is almost solid with weed, yet carp to nearly 40lbs are landed from there. Buoyant or semi-buoyant baits may do well when there is a weed carpet which stretches from one inch to a foot from the bottom. Reeds can actually cut line, so be careful when fishing amongst them. *Very* thick water lilies will defeat the strongest tackle, so steer clear of these if you can.

Writing for advice: always enclose a stamped addressed envelope when asking for advice, help or information. If you do not, you should not expect a reply. And don't expect well-known anglers to tell you about waters near your home; *you* live in the area, so you go out and find them!

It is pointless also to ask for a bait recipe, as so many people do. I could send anyone one of the recipes for a bait which is working on my waters, but there is no guarantee that it would succeed on any other. It might fail for a number of reasons: because it has already been used, the carp have been caught on it, and are 'off' it; because the angler concerned didn't use it in the right way; because he didn't fish often enough or persist with the bait long enough, and so on.

If the bait did not succeed, then the angler concerned might say that he was given a 'useless' recipe, and he may even write and accuse the person who gave him the recipe of misleading him! I know, for this actually happened to me, and for this reason I will not now send people bait recipes. Those who don't like carp anglers are only too anxious to accuse them of excessive secrecy, but as you can see from the above, that is often not the reason for not giving out information.

The Kevin Maddocks Specialist Bait range is available in Savoury, Citrus and Marine versions. These easily prepared nutritious baits contain a balance of proteins and vitamins together with special search and taste stimulators making them highly attractive to carp. On the reverse of each packet there are directions for making paste, boilies or floaters and these baits will not only attract the fish, they can achieve total pre-occupation if used correctly. Blended by British Groundbaits to my exact specification and available from all leading angling shops together with a free advisory pamphlet.

The Carp Anglers' Association

The CAA was founded in 1974 with 60 members, and now it has over 1,500. There are members throughout this country, and in eleven other countries also. Membership is open to all; there are no entry qualifications. Send your entry fee and annual subscription to CAA Headquarters (see address list at the back of this book), and you are a member. At present, CAA membership costs £8 (£1 entry fee and £7 annual subscription). For those who are under 16, full membership is available for £5, with no entry fee.

The CAA is an independent, non-political, social organisation with no rules or regulations. No-one will tell you what to do once you are a member, although we hope that all our members will be responsible anglers who are well behaved when they go fishing, who will be keen on conserving the fish they catch and the countryside they fish in and who will be helpful to others.

The CAA does not take part in angling politics; it is not affiliated to any other organisation which has rules to which members might not agree, and the subscriptions of its members, and the time of its organisers, is devoted to working for the members themselves, and not to involvement in angling 'politics'. This means that at CAA meetings and Conferences the talk will be of carp and carp fishing, although we will, of course, represent **those who join us** at any level and in any way they may require.

We do not attempt to represent those who do not join us; this is why CAA meetings, and CAA magazines, are for members only. There are said to be 20,000 people who go carp fishing in this country. Of these, only about 1,500 join carp fishing organisations. Neither we, nor anyone else, can 'represent' those who do not join us, nor can we pretend to be doing anything to help carp anglers in general. There is, in fact, no such thing as 'carp fishing' (in inverted commas). There are all the thousands who fish for carp, and there are the comparatively few who join the CAA, and who are therefore part of carp fishing organisation, which was started by the BCSG and the CAA between 1969 and 1974. It would be quite wrong to say that we are in any way representing those who will not join us, and for that matter I cannot think of one aspect of so called 'angling politics' which would be agreed to by every carp angler in the country. Anyone who doubts this should try to get a group of carp anglers together to discuss any of the burning topics of the day in connection with angling – there will not be much agreement!

I feel that national one-species organisations such as the CAA should be social organisations devoted to helping and providing information for their members; those who wish to take part in angling politics can do so through membership of the National Anglers Council, the Angling Co-operative Association (anti-pollution), or through their own angling clubs.

The CAA has branches throughout the country, each with a local Branch Secretary. Dozens of local meetings of from 20 to 100 members are held, probably some of which are in your area. These range from a social get-together in a pub to talk about carp fishing informally, to large meetings in halls with well known carp anglers as speakers, tackle displays, films etc.

At the last CAA national Conference, which was held in Dunstable, Beds., there were nearly 700 members who attended, and a large tackle show where you could see and buy tackle, baits and bait materials. Many of the leading carp anglers in the country are CAA members, and were present at this Conference.

There are regular magazines, including 'The Carp Catcher', our full colour magazine, which is sent free to all members three times a year, while members can obtain advice and assistance in connection with carp fishing either from CAA/HQ, or from local Branch Secretaries. Members range from complete beginners to nationally known carp anglers like Kevin Maddocks, who is joint Branch Secretary with John Baker for the Lea Valley CAA Branch, and is also Assistant Editor of the magazine 'The Carp Catcher'.

There are many other advantages of CAA membership, and I strongly advise all readers of this book to join, if they are not already members; CAA membership will do much to help you with your carp fishing, and eventually perhaps you, too, will wish to contribute to our magazine and to help others at meetings and Conferences.

A CAA member has a carp fishing friend in almost any part of the country to which he may travel, and this applies in a number of other countries also. As a further inducement to join, the CAA Secretary runs a number of syndicate carp waters, and CAA members have a good chance of being able to join one of these!

Glossary of Carp Fishing Terms

Bivvy: from bivouac; shelter, usually placed over an umbrella.

Betalight: small light source, filled with tritium gas. Ideal for attaching to bite indicators or floats.

Bite-off: when carp bites through line with throat (pharyngeal) teeth.

Blank (*1*): prepared material, split cane, glass or carbon fibre, from which rod is made.

Blank (*2*): session when no fish are caught; or, more correctly, when none are even hooked.

Bobbin: common but incorrect name for bite indicator hung on the line.

Boilie: boiled bait, mixed with eggs.

Bolt rig: terminal tackle designed to cause carp to bolt.

Bomb: Arlesey bomb leger weight.

BCSG: British Carp Study Group.

Buzzer: any type of electric or electronic bite indicator.

CAA: Carp Anglers' Association.

Cabbages: thick water lilies which don't normally grow to the surface.

Cloop: sucking noises made by protractile lips of carp (and other species) when taking surface baits; hence 'clooper'.

Controller: type of 'float' on line to aid casting distance with light surface fished baits, but intended mainly as a floating 'weight', and not as a visible float.

Churner: fast carp-take which spins (or 'churns') the reel handle when the bale arm is closed, and the anti-reverse off.

Cruiser: carp surface cruising, usually in hot weather and often with back out of the water.

Deucer: Norfolk term for double.

Double: carp weighing 10lbs or more.

Drag: undertow which pulls line into a bow, causing indicators to lift; best cured by line clips.

Drop: distance between the rod when in rests and the bite indicator on the line.

Drop-back bite: occurs when indicator drops, instead of 'going up', or line falls slack between rod tip and water.

Feeding take: slow, sometimes jerky, but confident take.

Floater: any floating bait.

Hair: rig in which bait is not on the hook (see text).

High protein (*bait*): bait with a high protein content, usually about 60% protein content or more, which can only normally be achieved by using sodium caseinate, casein, or calcium caseinate (Casilan).

HNV bait: this stands for High Nutritional (or Nutritive) Value. These are similar to HP baits, but the term recognises the fact that to be highly nutritional a bait (or food) need not necessarily have a high protein content.

Kiting: this occurs when a hooked carp bolts towards and to one side of the angler who is playing it on a tight line (more common at long range).

Line bite: movement of the indicator when a fish brushes line; can also be caused by a water vole or a bat!

Maggot basher: small fish angler.

Multiple baits: small baits such as sweet corn, beans, peas, etc.

Needle: metal rod on which bite indicator, after being attached to line, is mounted.

Noddy: mildly insulting term for inexperienced carp angler or non-carp angler (not, of course, to be applied to readers of this book!). Sometimes called 'Nodbo' in the south east.

Optonic: type of electronic bite indicator, or 'buzzer'.

Parrot mouth: carp with corners of mouth torn away by constant hooking and careless unhooking.

Particle bait: see 'multiple baits'.

Pharynged: term coined to describe bite-offs.

Pitch: carp fishing spot, or swim.

Pre-occupation: when carp are feeding on a food, usually natural but sometimes a bait, to the extent that they ignore most other foods and baits.

Plook: short cast, usually performed underhand.

Rig: terminal tackle.

Run: carp bite.

Screamer: fish which takes very quickly, tearing line from spool.

Side strain: holding carp with rod tip close to the water and to one side of the angler, to prevent fish from reaching snag.

Applying side strain to turn the fish from weed or snags.

Shock leader: length of heavier line attached to the end tackle to absorb the shock of a very hard cast.

Spitting: when carp takes bait into lips and immediately ejects it.

Sodium caseinate: soluble milk product in powder form; more than 90% protein content; 'sticky' and useful as a 'binder'.

Take: carp run or bite.

Tenting: carp which pushes up weed or lilies with its back, thus betraying its presence.

Terylene link: short length of Terylene, braided line, or other soft line attached to the hook to prevent carp from feeling the stiffness of monofilament nylon.

Twitch: short take, often of only a few inches or so; hence 'twitcher'. Usually caused by fish moving bait a short distance, then ejecting it.

Wildie: original wild carp, of which there are now few left in this country.

Useful Addresses

BK Publishers, 103 Worcesters Avenue, Enfield, EN1 4ND.
British Carp Study Group, Heywood House, Pill, Bristol, BS20 0AE.
Carp Anglers' Association HQ, Heywood House, Pill, Bristol, BS20 0AE, tel. Pill 2129; *London Office:* 103 Worcesters Avenue, Enfield, EN1 4ND; *W. Midlands Office:* 372 Chester Road, Sutton Coldfield, Birmingham, tel. 021-373 6627 (daytime); *E. Midlands Office:* 15 Manor Way, Higham Ferrers, Northants, tel. 0933-314395.

*   *   *   *   *

Anglers Co-operative Association, Midland Bank Chambers, Westgate, Grantham, Lincs. (anti-pollution organisation).
National Anglers Council, 11 Cowgate, Peterborough, tel. 0733 54084.
British Record Fish Committee, 11 Cowgate, Peterborough, tel. 0733 54084.
Infectious Diseases Laboratory, Weymouth, tel. 72137.
Anglers Mail (weekly), Kings Reach Tower, Stamford Street, London, SE1 9LS, tel. 01-261 6025.
Angling Times (weekly), Bretton Court, Bretton, Peterborough, PE3 8DZ, tel. 0733 266222.
Coarse Angler, 281 Eccleshall Road, Sheffield, S11 8NX, tel.0742 686132.
Coarse Fisherman, 32 Daventry Road, Norton, Daventry, Northants., tel. 03272 4751.

*   *   *   *   *

Fox International (KM Adjusta-level bedchair), 56-58 Fowler Road, Hainault Industrial Estate, Hainault, Essex IG6 3UT, tel. 01-501 0921/6.

Duncan Kay's Angling Services (carp bait, bait ingredients, flavours, tackle), 15 Manor Way, Higham Ferrers, Northants., tel. 0933 314395.

Geoff Kemp Bait Ingredients (flavours, bait and bait materials), Pilgrims Court, Days Lane, Pilgrims Hatch, Brentwood, Essex, tel. 0277 7429.

Bait '78 (bait, bait materials, flavours and tackle), 103 Chingford Mount Road, Chingford, London, E4, tel. 01-531 45199.

Terry Eustace Tackle (Terry Eustace Carp Rods and all tackle), 372 Chester Road, Sutton Coldfield, Birmingham, tel. 021-373 6627.

Simpsons of Turnford (KM Carbon Carp Rods and all other tackle), Nunsbury Drive, Turnford, Broxbourne, Herts., tel. Hoddesdon 468799.

Alan Brown Rod Developments (all tackle), 118 Nightingale Road, Hitchin, Herts., tel. 59918.

Veals Fishing Tackle (Paul Hughes) (Peter Mohan Carp Rods and all tackle), 61 Old Market Street, Bristol 2, tel. 0272 20790/291788.

Bruce Ashby Carp Rods, 223 Maidstone Road, Rainham, Kent, tel. Medway 33569.

Trevor Moss, The Tackle Shop, 42 Tooley Street, Gainsborough, Lincs., tel. 0427 3002.

Delkim Developments (Del Romang) (specialist electronic bite indicators, carp sacks and CB (Chris Brown) tackle), 27 Lea Road, Benfleet, Essex, tel. 03745 58013.

Kevin Nash, 'Happy Hooker Products' (carp sacks, weighing slings and tackle), 5 Silverdale, Rayleigh, Essex, tel. 0268 770238.

Kent Angling (Peter Henton) (all tackle), Unit N3, London Road Industrial Estate, London Road, Sittingbourne, Kent, tel. 0795 26011.

Leadbarrows (all tackle), 198 Church road, Urmston, Manchester, M31 1DX, tel. 061-748 0959.

Ampthill Aquatics, Sewardstone Road, Chingford, London, E4, tel. 01-524 4374 (lily removal, netting service).

Brian Mills Wood Carvings (authentic wood carvings of fish, already stocked by Harrods), 3 West Dumpton Lane, Ramsgate, Kent, tel. 0843 581177.
British Groundbaits (Kevin Maddocks Specialist Baits), Bardfield Saling, Nr. Braintree, Essex, tel. 0371 850247.

Spawning day for landing nets! From left to right the author's 36 inch stalking net with laminated ash arms, made for him by Rex Elgood, of Lincoln; the big Mike Starkey net; and Simpson's KM stalking net.